Mary Hartley is a writer, presenter and personal development coach specialising in people skills and communication. She has published a range of books on stress management, assertiveness, managing anger and listening skills and has been widely quoted in leading newspapers and magazines as well as appearing on radio and television shows.

Mary's books offer practical realistic advice and include self-assessment materials, exercises and practical tips to increase your confidence and self-esteem. They focus on ways of developing a positive style of behaviour based on self-respect and respecting others.

Mary Hartley's published books include: *The Good Stress Guide, How to Listen, How To Cope With Stress At Work, How To Cope With Anger at Work, The Assertiveness Handbook, A Guide to Anger Management, The Busy Woman's Handbook* and *Body Language at Work.*

The Smart Girl's Guide to Getting What You Want

HOW TO BE ASSERTIVE WITH WIT, STYLE AND GRACE

MARY HARTLEY

WATKINS PUBLISHING
LONDON

This edition published in the UK 2014 by
Watkins Publishing Limited, Sixth Floor,
75 Wells Street, London W1T 3QH

A member of Osprey Group

Design and typography Copyright © Watkins Publishing Limited, 2014
Text Copyright © Mary Hartley, 2014

Mary Hartley has asserted her right
under the Copyright, Designs and Patents Act 1988 to be
identified as the author of this work.

1 3 5 7 9 10 8 6 4 2

Design and typesetting by Paul Saunders

Printed and bound in the UK by CPI Group (UK) Ltd, Croydon, CR0 4YY

A CIP record for this book is available from the British Library

ISBN: 978-1-78028-554-2

www.watkinspublishing.co.uk

Contents

·

CHAPTER ONE

What is a Smart Girl?

A SMART GIRL, no matter what her age, is one who has learnt from her years on this planet. She has learnt it is vital to establish and develop sound and fulfilling relationships in every area of life. She has learnt to embrace opportunities to connect with other people without being scared to speak or take the initiative. She takes responsibility for her actions and her words. She is comfortable in her own skin and will take risks, secure in the knowledge that if something does go wrong, positive communication can put it right. And she knows the gifts of grace and confidence are not bestowed on us at birth by some kindly fairy godmother but are skills and approaches that she can learn and develop. Discovering fabulous ways of communicating is exciting and challenging. It's one of the thrills of being grown-up, and will enhance your life and your relationships.

Why assertiveness is smart

Assertiveness is a way of behaving and communicating that is based on acceptance of oneself and of other people. It demonstrates confidence without being overconfident, and self-control without trying to control others.

It shows you respect yourself and you respect other people as well – in fact, you respect others too much to play games with them or to patronise them by assuming they cannot take dissent or disagreement.

When you behave assertively, you are open and honest without hurting or diminishing others. You put forward your opinions and needs without putting yourself up on centre stage.

This behaviour is smart because it shows a high degree of self-awareness and self-knowledge and a willingness to engage honestly with other people. You know that there is nothing to lose and everything to gain from being open and upfront. You are not scared to put yourself out there.

We are all social beings and other people's opinion and perception of you matter but you are at the stage in life, either in years or mentality or both, where you can take responsibility for yourself. You are not cowed into behaving in certain ways because you worry what someone will think of you because you are confident enough to be true to yourself.

You acknowledge and own your feelings without trying to place the responsibility or blame for them on to other people.

Being assertive enables you to live a grown-up life, with all the challenges, enjoyments and contradictions that may involve.

And you can do it with style.

Why we find it hard to be assertive

You think it means being aggressive ...

It is easy to see why you might think this. The word 'assertive' is often wrongly used to describe forceful, dominant behaviour which may have toppled off the high end of the assertiveness scale and become aggressive.

We will look more closely at the crucial differences in these two styles of behaviour but bear in mind that assertive behaviour is inclusive of others' needs and positions, whereas aggressive behaviour is blind to anyone else's feelings, words or situation.

Aggressive responses tend not to be thought-out. They are instinctive reactions, sometimes very healthy ones, like the yell you give if you see someone trying to make off with your bag, or the bellow you did not know you had in you when you want to stop a child running across the road. That's fine.

In most circumstances, however, more controlled responses are more appropriate. Sometimes, the line between assertion and aggression is thin, but stay on the right side of it and you will not be perceived as aggressive. You are a smart girl, not a pushy cow.

You want to be liked ...

It is only natural to want people to like us. None of us wants to be Jenny No-Mates. Our natural desire from babyhood onward is to be accepted and to be part of a group. As for the benefits of friendship, many of us value and nurture our close relationships and our friendships more with each passing day, and we don't want to do anything to jeopardise them. So we feel we cannot do or say anything we think might contradict or upset someone else and this perception puts a stranglehold on our behaviour.

But upping your input in an assertive way won't turn people away: it will help to forge stronger connections. Anxiety about being liked can make us behave in quite un-smart ways such as not opening our mouths in case we offend someone, behaving in a way we think will get approval and please other people, never refusing a request and never asking for anything in case we put someone out.

If you take this to the extreme so it becomes a way of life, you could end up relinquishing all control over your actions and becoming a liability to yourself. The fear of not being liked could rob you of the ability to respond honestly and independently, which may be frustrating not only for you but for the people you deal with as well.

The desire to be nice and to be liked can be self-defeating as you may irritate and frustrate those who would welcome a positive response and find wimpish, lukewarm communication just plain annoying.

You don't want to be rude …

Of course you don't want to be rude! Smart girls dislike impolite, thoughtless or ungracious behaviour. They would never behave in this way (or if they do, they apologise and make amends pretty quickly).

We need to pause and think about the use of the word 'rude' in this context. We probably mean behaviour that is not polite and that is socially unacceptable. It is likely that we use the word in a variety of contexts, some of which reflect our own views and some of which reflect ideas about behaving nicely which we received when we were children:

+ *It's rude to stare.*

+ *It's rude to contradict.*

+ *It's rude to speak with your mouth full.*

+ *It's rude to push in.*

Some of these examples do indicate lack of courtesy or consideration for others, which is what rudeness or impoliteness is all about. But one of these activities may actually be done assertively and graciously – the second on the list. It is *not* rude to contradict or disagree. It may be done in a rude fashion, as is the case with anything we say, but it doesn't need to be. Disagreeing with someone or pointing out mistakes in what he or she says may be an appropriate response and may be done without showing disrespect for the speaker. It is also a vital part of lively discussion and conversation.

You might find it helpful to rethink some of your assumptions about 'rude' behaviour. Assertiveness considers other people and is the opposite of rudeness. Assertive behaviour shows respect.

You feel uncomfortable about the idea that you have rights ...

Assertive behaviour is often described as standing up for your rights. Well, this concept is at the heart of assertion and it is a good description of the basic attitude that informs assertive behaviour. You need to accept the fact that you have all kinds of rights you can claim. You have the right to ask for what you want, to express your feelings, to change your mind, to make a joke, to be nasty to someone if that's what you choose to do – the list goes on. You have the right to choose from the whole range of communicative behaviour.

The trouble is we sometimes feel uncomfortable with this idea. Perhaps we think it has a strident ring. We feel it can sound a little 'in-your-face', a bit like the women in *Made in Dagenham* (2010) but without the backcombed hair and A-line skirts (we're not saying that was a bad look, *au contraire*). Having rights need not mean claiming them vigorously and vociferously in every situation. What it *does* mean is you have a bedrock of security which enables you to make good choices about how you behave.

If the particular word 'right' doesn't sit easily with you, modify it a little. Tell yourself:

+ *I'm grown-up now, and I can say this.*

+ *It's OK to feel like this, and it's OK to express these feelings.*

+ *It's actually all right to value my opinions, my needs, my judgements.*

Another way of thinking which you might find helpful is to refer to the context in which you are exercising your 'right' to speak and behave in a particular way:

+ *It's a mark of a good friend to say when something is wrong.*

+ *It's a mark of a good professional to be able to refuse or to make work-related requests.*

+ *It's a mark of an emotionally healthy person to express anger.*

Whatever you think or feel, it is OK. Your opinions are yours. You can choose to share them, or not. Other people may disagree or find them hard to understand. That's fine. They are entitled to their thoughts and feelings, just as you are to yours. In the grown-up world, we can handle differences. Are you obliged to justify your feelings or your opinions? No. You don't *have* to. You may *choose* to – that is entirely up to you.

What a smart girl never, ever, forgets is everyone else has these rights as well.

You think there's no point ...

You know the feeling. We tell ourselves it is pointless to say anything because no one will listen or nothing will change. We think of all the effort involved in developing new ways of behaviour and decide it just is not worth it. It is too much hassle and it is not going to make any difference anyway.

This is something of a cop-out. By convincing ourselves that changing the way we approach a person or a situation would be a useless course of action, we allow ourselves to slump back into unproductive and personally harmful patterns of behaviour. You are also making assumptions about how other people will react, without giving them the opportunity to adjust to a different scenario.

It *is* worth giving it a go. It *is* worth giving the people in your life a chance to see a situation through new eyes and benefit from positive dialogue. It *is* worth making the effort to improve the quality of your communication and your relationships, and to feel good about yourself.

You think you shouldn't have to say anything ...

We get hung up on the idea, although logic tells us it is ridiculous, that people should know what we are thinking and what we want without being told. While it is true that in close and intimate relationships we can sometimes read each other's minds and predict reactions and behaviours, it doesn't follow we are justified in feeling put out and aggrieved when things don't work out that way.

Perhaps everyone should know that when we say yes, we really mean no, that we are not happy with a suggestion or that we are angry. Maybe they should, but they don't. Maybe we should not have to spell things out, but if we just decide to do it, at least there is no room for misunderstanding.

You assume negative consequences ...

You worry about how people are going to react, and you always anticipate the worst outcome. You are running scared all the time: if I say this, I'll lose my job, this person will never speak to me again, I'll be laughed at, that person will be really upset, I'll never be able to come to this place again, the world will end, and so on. This is a pattern of thinking which has become a habit, and it is a habit that you can break.

You think it is unfeminine ...

This is one we really need to get straight. Since when has behaving in a courteous, straightforward, pleasant and appropriate manner been unfeminine? Is it unfeminine to show empathy? To show thoughtfulness? To chat and joke? To stand your ground when someone gets at you? To ask for a pay rise? What image of femininity do you have?!

There was a time, way back when women were discouraged from expressing their feelings, from competing in the workplace, from being anything other than a caregiver and nurturer. We were expected to be 'sugar and spice and all things nice'.

We know better now. We know that being feminine is *not* about being compliant and helpless. We know that it is *not* about being scared to speak up. We know that it is *all* about being confident in our skins.

You may well find that those who say assertive behaviour is unfeminine are those who feel threatened by your grown-up presence and are looking for a way to undermine you.

You don't know how to ...

Perhaps you feel you want to handle situations differently but you don't know what to say. You would like to express yourself more clearly and honestly but you cannot get the right words. You want to sound authoritative and you end up sounding abrupt. You want to sound angry and you come across squeaky and petulant. You open your mouth to say no and find yourself agreeing to everything.

Behaving assertively is a skill you can learn. It is not easy and it is not automatic. Once upon a time, when you were very, very young, you didn't need to think about it, and had no problem letting people know when you were upset, hungry or happy. A lot of socialisation has gone on since then and our instinctive responses have become more controlled and sophisticated.

This is a good thing but it does mean we need to make a conscious effort to express ourselves appropriately, which involves developing new attitudes and learning specific techniques.

Even then, it is not easy. We need to practise, possibly get it wrong now and again, but to be able to pick ourselves up and start over. Human interaction is complex and amazing and surprising and there is no guarantee that we will always get it right. But the continued effort to get it as right as we can is a challenging and rewarding learning process that never ends.

Why it is worth developing an assertive approach

You will get better relationships in every area of your life. Your confidence and self-esteem will increase and you will feel really good about yourself. This is not because you will always get your way – assertiveness is not about winning

– but because when you behave with integrity and thoughtfulness, other people treat you with liking and respect.

Often, it is not the big issues that concern us but the ordinary, everyday situations we don't handle as confidently and effectively as we would like. You want to be able to say no when your best friend asks if she can borrow your new top, your son wants to use your car or your daughter wants you to look after her children for the third time this week. You wish you knew what to say when your boss asks you to take on extra work that you don't want to do. You'd like to be able to tell the person who decorated your kitchen that the paintwork is sloppy. You'd like to be able to tell the man over the road who you have never spoken to that you love what he has done with his garden, instead of just thinking it, and you would have felt so good if you'd had the courage to suggest a coffee meeting to that interesting woman you met at the fund-raiser. You'd love to be able to say you don't want a family holiday this year. Oh, and you'd love to be able to say something to the people whose talking at the cinema spoils your enjoyment of the film …

It's the little things, and they add up. The little things that you don't handle well all accumulate so you end up living a life that is less confident, less inclusive, less vibrant, less fun than it need be. Smart girl, you are worth more!

Here are just some of the things you will be able to do:

+ Say no to things you don't want to do.

+ Ask for things you want.

+ Start conversations.

✦ Take friendships a stage further.

✦ Be criticised without getting upset (not too much, anyway!).

✦ Be critical of other people without wrecking the relationship.

✦ Say nice things to people without sounding insincere.

✦ Be gracious when people say nice things to you.

✦ Disagree without being 'in-your-face' or so timid that you are not noticed.

✦ Know when to speak and when to shut up.

✦ Deal with put-downs.

✦ Apologise appropriately.

Isn't this person someone you'd like to be your best friend? Isn't she someone you'd like to work with, or for? Someone you would love to be in your family circle? Someone you trust, someone whose company you enjoy? Of course she is. This person isn't just assertive – this person is a goddess.

And *you* can be one, too.

CHAPTER TWO

The Bulldozer, the Pushover, the Snake – and the Star

Different styles of behaviour

Many of us exhibit patterns of behaviour that are predictable and consistent. You can probably identify someone you deal with who is always moaning, someone who will never make a decision or someone who challenges every remark.

Picture this situation:

You're out for a meal with a group of friends and the service is poor. Everyone is annoyed about this.

One of the group feels she would like to complain but doesn't want to make a fuss.

Another tells the waiter he should get another job if this is the best he can do.

Another smiles sweetly at the waiter, tells him it is no problem and decides to get back at the place by posting a bad review online.

Or this one:

Someone at work or in a social group expresses views that the others find offensive.

One of the group laughs uncertainly.

Another tells the speaker to shut up.

Another nods and smiles as if agreeing, then slags off the speaker behind his back.

Do you recognise these patterns? Maybe you can identify friends and family members who would be likely to respond in these ways.

Maybe you can recognise yourself.

There is no right or wrong in these kinds of behaviour. If the way you behave represents the way you want to be, that is your choice. But if you would like to respond differently, it is helpful to start by recognising any patterns that have developed and find ways of altering your automatic reaction so you learn to say what you would *really* like to say, and learn to say it in a way which makes you feel good and does not damage other people. Speaking in a different way will seem strange at first, but once you get used to it, you will love your new confident voice.

The bulldozer

Do you recognise this person?

Here we have the person whose aggressive behaviour often intimidates you, the person you wish you could stand up to but feel you haven't got the confidence or the know-how to deal with.

Use the following descriptions to help you recognise and understand this behaviour pattern. Recognition and understanding will give you a strong foundation from which you can develop effective strategies for dealing with pushy people. Someone who behaves like a bulldozer could be described in some of these ways:

+ Impatient

+ Argumentative

+ Likes to tell people what to do

+ Hostile

+ Forceful

+ Insensitive

+ Always right

+ Sarcastic

+ Pushy

+ Putting people on the spot

What this behaviour is like

People who behave in this punchy, aggressive way are out to get their own way regardless of what other people think, do or say. They send the message that their needs are more important than anyone else's. Their behaviour shows a lack of respect for others. At worst, this person can come across as a bit of a bully.

Nancy Sinatra, lovely daughter of the fabulous Frank, memorably sang that one of these days her boots would walk all over you. She made it sound strong and sexy. But when you are the one on the receiving end, it is not so great.

However, you can deal with it, you really can. The first thing to do is to recognise this pattern of behaviour. Take a deep breath, stand back and see if any of the following examples are familiar.

Pushing to get their own way

For these people, the right result is the one that they want, and they go all out to get it. This might mean pushing and badgering until you cave in. You know what it is like when you just feel too exhausted to argue any more and agree to anything to get someone off your back.

Sometimes bulldozers use threats and state or imply it is in your best interests to agree with their demands. If you don't agree, they override your wishes and go ahead with what they want to do anyway. They don't let anything go. Winning is all that matters, so they make sure they always have the last word and that there is no doubt about who has emerged on top.

Signature sentence – If they don't like it, they'll just have to get on with it.

Being inflexible

Bulldozers give the impression that negotiation and compromise are not in their vocabulary. They see things in black and white, and they know which side they are on. For them, there are only winners and losers, and any concessions are a sign of weakness. They attack and undermine alternative views and see others' attempts to discuss or talk things over as invitations to fight. They are the only ones who are allowed to be right.

Signature sentence – It's my way or the highway.

Not listening

Because their agenda is to get what they want, they are not interested in other people's views or feelings. They may pretend to be listening but their attention is elsewhere. Often, they butt in and talk over the other person.

Signature sentence – Yeah, yeah, whatever.

Using sarcasm and put-downs as a means of control

There is nothing funny or well meant about their use of these tactics. We are not talking about shared teasing and joking between friends here but about comments that are intended to hurt and to demonstrate someone's superiority while putting others down.

Signature sentence – You would say that, wouldn't you?

Presenting opinions as if they are undeniable facts

Bulldozers believe they are right, so they definitively declare 'That's rubbish!' or 'That will never work!' They don't see themselves as opinionated, they see themselves as right.

Signature sentence – What a ridiculous thing to say!

Using speech as a blunt instrument

Bulldozers sometimes shout or speak very loudly, and sometimes speak very, very quietly so that they sound a little threatening and others have to strain to hear them. They interrupt conversations and talk over people regardless of the circumstances – the most important thing is that they are heard. Their tone is harsh and strident, and they don't modulate it to suit the circumstance.

Aggressive body language

You can see this attitude in the way people walk. They stride purposefully with the air of being prepared to push everyone else out of the way. Their gestures are sharp and forceful, with lots of jabbing fingers and banging fists. They commandeer space in a way that intimidates and diminishes others. They take up more than your fair share of room.

Have you experienced the person who puts bags and belongings on the vacant seat beside him or her and ignores other people's indications that the seat is needed? This might just be thoughtless behaviour but often it is an aggressive strategy in which the spread-out items present a wordless challenge to anyone who might wish to use the claimed space.

There is a range of postures with which bulldozers emphasise their superiority, such as standing when someone is sitting or towering above them. They may come up too close to people, or lean over or across them.

They use eye contact to disconcert others. They stare steadily at someone in order to make them feel uncomfortable, and they are never the first to break a gaze.

Why people behave like this

They are not bad people. Not always. Perhaps the image of 1980s' power dressing has gone to their heads, or their shoulders, at any rate. Remember the big jackets with shoulders like American footballers' that practically came into the room before you, and the big hair to match, styled and moussed to make your head seem six times bigger than your body?

A bulldozer's behaviour does indicate an affinity with some of the attitudes of that decade when Michael Douglas as Gordon Gekko in the film *Wall Street* (1987) proclaimed that 'greed is good' and 'lunch is for wimps' and Madonna showed us all how to be Material Girls.

It could be that people who behave aggressively are not able to or have not learnt to control their automatic instincts. It could be their early-life experiences have taught them the best form of defence is attack. Maybe they feel insecure and behaving aggressively is the only way they can think of preventing others from seeing this. Or, perhaps, they just get it wrong – they mean to be forceful and come across as hostile.

It can happen to us all. We intend to ask a firm question and we sound like someone from the Spanish Inquisition. We make what is meant to be a joke and it sounds like a snide comment. We don't mean to be unpleasant, it is just that lack of skill and control has caused us to mismanage our communication.

Occasionally, the time and the place can have a negative influence on our behaviour. You know how we all can be at our worst in certain situations. It could be that particular circumstances bring out the attacking mode: a drink or three too many, feeling tired and scratchy, being angry and wound up about something. It can easily happen.

The trouble is, sometimes an aggressive approach is seen as the best way to get results. There are short-term gains when people like this are perceived as being successful and winners who get what they want. They may be viewed with admiration or a kind of uneasy respect. No one answers back or gives them a hard time because they are all just a little bit scared, wary or intimidated.

What bulldozers lose

This is not a winning approach. You might think that people who are too pushy come out on top, but they don't. Any gains they have from aggressive behaviour are shallow and short-lived. This approach does not lead to good relationships, it damages existing relationships and prevents people from developing positive connections.

Bulldozers alienate people and push them away, becoming detached and isolated in the process. When it is all about you and never about anyone else, people keep their distance and lose respect. And in the end, bulldozers lose respect for themselves as well.

Leading lady

The character Miranda Priestly in the film *The Devil Wears Prada* (2006). Powerful and ruthless, she subjects her young assistant to emotional and psychological bullying.

The pushover

Do you recognise this person?

You might see your own behaviour falling into this category. You may well feel unconfident and unable to deal with people you perceive to be more powerful or important than you, people you feel you cannot answer back or stand up to.

Perhaps you have fallen into a pattern of agreeing with and accepting things you don't like and feel that you cannot respond any differently. Believe me, you can break this pattern. Look at the following descriptions and think about what you would like to change, because you really *can* change.

Someone who behaves like a pushover could be described in some of these ways:

✦ Disliking conflict or unpleasantness

✦ Tending to go along with things

✦ Thinking that there is no point in rocking the boat

✦ Finding it easier to agree

✦ Believing it is important to be nice

✦ Liking to be helpful

✦ Liking to be liked

✦ Finding it hard to say no

✦ Doing anything for a quiet life

✦ Believing it is better not to say anything than to say
something that might upset someone

What this behaviour is like

Oh dear! The word pushover is a bit cruel, isn't it? It sounds
like the title of a film in which the main character is sub-
jected to lots of hilarious pratfalls. It implies that someone
is easily swayed, easily persuaded and easily forced into
doing things. But I'm being cruel to be kind because it
matters so much that you don't allow yourself to be beaten
down by other people's forceful or manipulative behaviour.

Actually, they don't even need to be particularly forceful
– the slightest nudge and you are on the ground, agreeing
with whatever is said and unable to express your feelings or
opinions, letting someone else take over and make the decisions, putting yourself last, imagining that the best way to
stay out of trouble and keep the peace is to keep your head
down and let other people have their own way. You might
as well go around with a sign on your back saying 'Kick me.'

Harsh words, I know, but dear Ms Soon-to-be ex-push-
over, we are looking at the most extreme manifestations of
this behaviour just to jolt you into realising that!

Saying yes when you really want to say no

'I'm just a girl who can't say no' – don't you just want to start
humming the tune from the musical *Oklahoma*? It is such
a little word, but we can find it so hard to say.

We agree to work late even though we had plans for the evening; we take on tasks that we really don't want to and don't have to do; we agree to go out in spite of a splitting headache; we lend our friend or our children money because we cannot refuse even though we are never paid back … oh, just think about all the situations in which we would love to be able to say no.

Sometimes, you'll agree to something while thinking, 'Why am I doing this?' But you make the judgement that it is the best thing to do in the circumstances. That is a gracious, grown-up choice. But your problem is that you cannot say no even when your heart and your head and everything else tell you what you should do is refuse.

Signature sentence – I didn't want to, but you can't say no, can you?

Not speaking up when something bothers you

You might decide to put up with life's minor irritations, and that is a very good idea. We can hardly get through a day without coming up against people who annoy us, and situations which get to us, and how exhausting would it be to take on each and every one.

It is fine to let go of the things that don't matter, but people whose behaviour is overpassive don't say a thing even when a situation really gets to them.

You are treated unfairly at work, someone pushes in front of you in a queue, and you are in a hurry because your parking ticket is running out; you are annoyed because your friend is always late; you are hurt because someone who should have known better forgets your birthday – and you don't say a word.

You might be fuming inside but you cover it up and pretend everything is fine. If you do express your feelings, it is to anyone other than the person responsible. You pour out your woes to a friend, a colleague, your family, your cat, your dog – in fact, anyone who will give you a sympathetic ear. But the suggestion that you could talk about the situation with the relevant person fills you with horror.

Signature sentence – It doesn't really bother me, so it's not worth saying anything.

Letting others make decisions

You know what it is like when people won't make a decision? Oh, I don't mind, they say when faced with a choice of anything from 'Would you like Thai, Chinese or Indian food this evening?' to 'Should we move house?'

This is fine when someone really doesn't care, when the decision is a comparatively trivial one or when you would actually like someone else to make a choice. However, there are lots of occasions when we *do* have a preference, but cannot bring ourselves to voice it in case it contradicts what someone else wants.

What we do here is shift all the responsibility on to other

people, knowing that we can blame them if the decision turns out to be wrong. We might even say something like 'Well, I had reservations about the idea, but didn't like to say.' This has the immediate effect of making people want to give us a smack.

Signature sentence – It's up to you, I don't mind.

Always apologising

Oh my, we just love to apologise! In *Love Story* (1970), the characters say, 'Love means never having to say you're sorry' (that is, if you could hear the words above your sobbing as Ali McGraw's loveliness just grew and grew as her illness took hold). For those of us who behave like pushovers, life means always having to say you're sorry.

Let's be fair, though: 'sorry' is a word that is rather hardwired into our communicative programming. We use it in all kinds of ways – as a filler, an interrupter, a lead-in, a get-out. Sometimes we mean it to be a genuine apology, sometimes it is just shorthand for something else.

If someone knocks your arm in a crowded place and causes you to spill a drink, you might well say 'sorry' at the same time as the other person. You are not apologising for being there or for thoughtlessly presenting an opportunity for someone to bump into you: you are using the word to mean 'That's all right.' We sometimes say 'sorry' to mean 'excuse me' when making our way past people. So the word has become weaker – but it also weakens you.

When you apologise every time you open your mouth, you are putting yourself down and diminishing the impact of what you have to say. You use the word so indiscriminately that it is difficult to distinguish a genuine, appropriate apology from a run-of-the-mill request. You sound as if you are asking permission to speak. You make it worse by piling on the words: *I'm ever so sorry*; *I'm really sorry*; *I'm really, really sorry*; *I'm terribly sorry to bother you …*

Signature sentence – No apologies for not repeating the word – you know what it is.

Being unable to handle criticism – giving it or taking it

Let's face it, no one likes being criticised, even when, or *especially* when, it is justified. If you are in pushover mode, you tend to interpret any negative feedback as an attack and take no notice of any positive observations.

If, for example, you ask someone if they think you look better in the flowery top or the striped one, whatever the answer, you think, 'That means the other one makes me look fat.' Even the mildest reproach cuts you to the bone. Someone says, 'You're late,' and you think, 'Yes, I'm late! I'm a terrible person! I can't even get here on time! I'm useless! I don't deserve to live!' When there is some truth in a negative comment, you use it to fuel and justify your low self-esteem.

When there is little or no truth in what is said, you

actually think, 'That might be right, because after all I'm pretty hopeless.' And before you know *where* you are, you are caught up in a cycle of wretchedness, and you start to model the negative behaviour.

And sometimes you feel so inadequate that the slightest perceived criticism or rebuff makes you want to burst into tears.

Signature sentence – If you can't say something nice, don't say anything.

Whispering, not talking

This is in both the physical and the metaphorical sense. People who want to keep a low profile speak quietly and hesitantly. They might do a lot of throat clearing and use fillers such as 'er' and 'um', 'kind of' and 'you know what I mean'. Their vocal style suggests they feel they have no right to speak at all.

You know what it is like when you are afraid of being seen as too direct. You go all round the houses to explain what you mean, to make a point or to ask for something.

Your perception that asking for anything is unacceptable leads you to phrase comments in a way which anticipates failure: 'I don't suppose' and 'I expect you don't…' Of course you do not want to be thought of as shouty and demanding, but your tentative way of speaking means that you make it easy for people to misunderstand your meaning, either genuinely or deliberately.

Passive body language

Have you ever been in a meeting where the person in the chair looks brightly round the room and says, 'Who's going to take the minutes?' Or at a makeover session where the presenter asks for a volunteer to strip off?

A common reaction is for everyone there to immediately lower their eyes to avoid eye contact and make themselves as small as possible in the hope that this makes them invisible.

This is the impression that pushovers give most of the time: that their aim is to go through life unnoticed without having to deal with or engage with other people. So they develop a walk that is more like a creep or a scuttle, with head lowered and eyes fixed on the ground, and small scurrying steps to get them from a to b as quickly and unobtrusively as possible. In extreme cases, if they had a choice, their eyes would rarely leave the ground as they find eye contact uncomfortable.

This kind of behaviour is characterised by nervous gestures like twiddling with hair or jewellery, covering up the mouth or touching the face. It is often accompanied by nervous laughter or giggles to cover up feelings of awkwardness. It is highly possible that you smile when you feel like crying or when you are hearing something critical, and what your smile is saying is 'Please like me'.

You show your desire to keep yourself safely removed from the rest of the world by creating 'barriers'. You might fold your arms or cross them over your chest. You feel comfortable if there is an object such as a table between you and the other person. Your handbag comes in useful here. You plonk it on your knee, on a seat or on a table and you feel protected. You give the impression that you want to keep the world at bay.

Why people behave like this

It is not because you are weak or scared. You have simply got into a pattern of behaviour that protects you, even if it doesn't work for you in a positive way. You may well have developed this kind of behaviour in response to messages you received earlier in life. You may have been given approval or rewards for being well-behaved, which usually translates as being quiet and compliant. (And who can blame parents or care-givers for valuing manageable behaviour?

There are stories we could tell about the offspring of libertarian parents … sorry, 60s' sisters. But you know who you are. You may have been encouraged to stifle negative emotions and keep them to yourself. Your behaviour may have been shaped by the 'keep a stiff upper lip' and 'don't make a fuss' school of thought.

In the short term, you avoid conflict and disagreement. You don't have to deal with other people's feelings or acknowledge your own. You may have a reputation for being easy-going and unlikely to kick up a fuss about anything, which makes you feel good about yourself.

It is possible that your air of helplessness makes people

want to protect you. The patterns of behaviour you have developed settle around you as cosily as a cashmere wrap on a chilly evening.

What pushovers lose

You can pay a high price for being what you think is nice. You are not hurting anyone and are making things easy for them. But you take the idea 'It's not all about you' to such an extreme that it is *never* about you, and you end up being walked all over.

You damage yourself and limit your chances of living a fulfilling life. Your habit of letting other people call the shots means your real self, your own unique personality, becomes weak and pale until you lose touch with and can hardly recognise who you really are.

When you never make a choice, voice an opinion, defend yourself or do anything that you think might displease someone, you start to inhabit a strange place in which your feelings and emotions exist in a kind of parallel world that is removed from your physical presence. You become a ghost, and we are not talking in the romantic, Patrick Swayze way.

You think you are keeping others happy and that you are removing hassle and conflict from situations, and you might even think that people should be grateful to you for making their lives easier. But has it occurred to you that you might be a source of tension and frustration because you never come clean about your preferences?

You show lack of respect not just for yourself but for everyone else as well – you assume they are unable to handle disagreement or difference of opinion or expressions of feelings. Your capacity for developing open and trusting relationships is limited.

Because you never express negative feelings you are likely to experience a build-up of frustration and resentment. You may explode one day, shocking all those around you who never realised what you were feeling, or you may continue to bottle up your emotions and risk damaging your health as well as your relationships.

Leading lady

The unnamed (that says it all) narrator in Daphne du Maurier's *Rebecca*: naïve, gauche and insecure, she is pushed around by her employer, her housekeeper and her husband.

The snake

Do you recognise this person?

You might not recognise this person because his or her behaviour is devious and hard to pin down. We are talking here about manipulative behaviour that lulls you into a false sense of security so you don't realise you are being twisted around someone's little finger. Because these people are not all shouty and sweary, it can be difficult to see they are aggressive. There are many ways to trample over people and grind them into the floor without showing your hand – so watch out.

Use the following descriptions to help you identify and thus arm yourself against the destructive consequences of this behaviour – and check to see whether you ever use these tactics yourself. They are not worthy of you.

Someone who behaves like a snake will show some of these characteristics:

✦ Turning on the charm to get what they want

✦ Deliberately messing up a job or a task to make a point

✦ Believing that flattery usually works

✦ Pushing people's buttons to get a result

✦ Making sure to come out of any situation looking good

✦ Making promises and not following through

✦ Believing it is effective to use hints and suggestions rather than be direct

✦ Getting back at people

✦ Shifting blame on to others

✦ Putting a spin on situations to gain the advantage

✦ Playing one person off against another. Giving put-downs disguised as jokes.

What this behaviour is like

This person should be marked 'Handle with care.' This behaviour may be described as manipulative or passive aggressive and this person is harder to handle than someone who is out-and-out aggressive as at least you can recognise that person as the enemy.

But snakes are the enemy within, the ones who attack from behind. They can be so subtle in their attacks that their victim does not realise what is going on and might even regard them as friends.

Snakes intend to get their own way without anyone realising this is their agenda. So their attacks are sugar-coated pills. The sugar is a lavish sprinkling of appealing behaviour: they seem caring, friendly, funny, supportive and actually might be these things, but only when it suits them. How do we recognise their friends? From the stab marks in their backs.

The silent treatment

You might have experienced the person who does silence big time, whose silence is so loud it deafens everyone within earshot. When you ask what is wrong, you get a shrug and a curt 'nothing' before he or she lapses into silence again.

This tactic keeps people on their toes and leads them to worry about what they might have done to upset you. It is a form of control and puts you in the dominant position.

Signature sentence – You say it loudest when
you say nothing at all.

Putting on a show

Oh, snakes know just how to turn it on, don't they! When
it suits their purpose, they switch on the tears. When a display of anger will get the desired result, they manufacture
a temper tantrum. The flounce, the door shut just quietly
enough not to be an outright slam – it is superbly done.

Snakes have had lots of practice. They know how to look
sympathetic when they could not care less, interested when
they are bored, amused when they are angry. They pretend
to be shy and vulnerable when they are nothing of the kind.
They make out they are being light-hearted and amusing
but their funny quip or one-liner masks their real hostility
or desire to put someone down.

Whatever façade they present, no one can see that,
behind it, their mind is racing away, assessing the effect,
planning the next move.

Signature sentence – No, of course I'm not upset.

The guilt trip

Snakes are skilled at this. They know how to make people
feel they have done something wrong. They know what to
say and how to behave to make you think you have hurt
them, disappointed them or let them or somebody else

down. They push the buttons, which will ignite feelings of guilt, inadequacy and selfishness in those who are ready to respond in this way. They exploit people's weaknesses and manipulate their emotions, making them feel responsible for others' feelings.

Signature sentence – No, it's all right if you can't give me a lift – it's only two miles to walk along that dark road and I'm sure it will stop raining soon.

Using underhand tactics

When it comes to sabotage, people like this could be running the War Office. Rather than come out with the fact that they don't want to do something, they keep the other person sweet by agreeing, then make sure that they wriggle out of doing it.

You have come across the person who says they will go to a meeting, a social event or give someone a lift, then at the last minute, oh dear, the car won't start! And it's just been serviced as well.

If they do take something on unwillingly, they make sure they will not be asked again by making a mess of it (for which someone else will be blamed) or missing the deadline (for which someone else will be blamed). Or they might just 'forget' and charm their way out of it.

Signature sentence – I'm so sorry, I didn't mean to keep you waiting/burn the dinner/delete your work.

Playing people off against each other

Such a clever ploy, this one! The snake can make everyone feel he or she is their best friend, and they don't realise that each and every one of them is being used. The snake puts people down to others, sometimes in such a subtle way that the listener thinks the snake is actually saying something complimentary. No one can ever trace the source of a malicious rumour to the snake, because after all, snakes are never nasty about anyone, are they?

The snake cleverly turns people against each other. Snakes talk to each behind the other's back and, from their position of control, watch the damage they cause their relationship.

> *Signature sentence* – You're the only person I can really trust with this (said to several people).

A voice dripping with honey ...

... or it is lowered in a conspiratorial way, or it is a moan. Snakes choose the way they speak to get the result they desire. They could never be accused of speaking without thinking; every word is weighed and calculated. If it suits them to be friendly, they will adopt a warm and open tone; if they are playing games of exclusion or divide and rule, they will speak with meaningful nods and grimaces.

Manipulative body language

People who act like snakes control their non-verbal signals to create particular effects. Female snakes can be flirty and touchy-feely; they sometimes use cutesy infantile gestures and postures to give the impression of being just a harmless little girl. Male snakes stick to the flirty.

Many snakes have a range of facial expressions to indicate feelings without having to actually voice them – they are good at the raised eyebrow, often behind someone's back, the quick little frown or the dismissive shrug.

Why people behave like this

Not all snakes are poisonous or dangerous. Some people keep them as pets. Snake-like behaviour does not indicate a bad person, just someone who does what works and may not even have thought about alternatives. If this is you, you might have low self-esteem and an ill-defined sense of yourself.

Because of this you need to feel liked, loved and accepted, and you use manipulative tactics to avoid the possibility of rejection. You have a strong drive to control, but mask this by employing a range of strategies to make you seem appealing.

You manage the impression you create so that other people find you accessible and non-threatening, and they play back to you a flattering picture of yourself. It is nice to be popular and well liked. You get your own way without having to engage in honest, and possibly difficult, communication, and you protect yourself from arguments and unpleasantness.

What snakes lose

Sadly, snakes lose out in many ways. Although they seem to be always on top of their game, the games they play are likely to backfire at some point. They live on a knife edge, always on the verge of discovery, never sure when the moment will come for their victims to finally see through their ploys and challenge them to an honest conversation. People can feel unsettled and confused when they are around a manipulator and may avoid having to deal with them.

If this type of behaviour is habitual, you can reach the point where you are so out of touch with your real self and your real feelings that you find it difficult to identify them or to express them.

Your relationships may lack emotional depth. You miss out on the pleasures and satisfactions of engaging with people openly and honestly. Your favourite techniques and strategies give you a precarious hold on situations but you limit your emotional growth and you isolate yourself from others.

Leading lady

The character Eve Harrington in the film *All about Eve* (1950). She insinuates herself into Bette Davis's life and, while pretending to be a worshipping admirer, sets out to wreck Davis's career and steal her man.

The star

Do you recognise this person?

Here is the star, not in a goody-goody, always right way, far from it, but the person you like to deal with, the person you respect and trust, the person *you* yourself can be.

Someone whose behaviour is assertive could be described in some of these ways:

✦ Good at active listening

✦ Empathetic

✦ Looking for solutions

✦ Feeling confident in themselves

✦ Happy with their level of self-esteem

✦ Able to let people know what they want

✦ Able to express emotions

✦ Respecting themselves and others

✦ Able to handle conflict

✦ Able to give criticism or say negative things

✦ Able to deal with being on the receiving end of criticism or negative comments

What this behaviour is like

You choose the way you behave. This is not to say you are never spontaneous or you are always totally self-controlled – that wouldn't be any fun for you or anyone else. But you realise that no one is forcing you to behave in a particular way, and you take responsibility for your own actions.

You can make a choice about whether to confront a difficult situation or person, or to let it go. You can choose whether to complain about something or ignore it. You can choose whether to talk about your feelings or your beliefs, or to keep them to yourself.

The important thing is that these are choices made out of confidence, not fear. You have the self-knowledge to recognise if you are ducking away from a situation because you are scared and intimidated or because you have made a genuine choice.

You are confident in the whole range of situations that call for different levels of assertive behaviour. Many of us feel comfortable dealing with certain people but are unable to present the same behaviour in other circumstances. We can complain about faulty goods in a shop but when we don't like the way our hair's been cut, we nod and simper approvingly as our hairdresser shows us the back and side views. We can correct wrong information given by one of our family, while in a social group we keep quiet, or the other way round. We can ask our house- or flat-sharer to take their turn putting out the bins but cannot ask our work colleague to clear away the food debris they leave lying around.

You, however, are not intimidated by anyone. There are some people and situations you find tricky and demanding but you are able to express yourself appropriately to everybody you deal with.

Your confidence, self-awareness and self-esteem enable you to explore the whole gamut of behavioural styles. You can be playful, flirty, cheeky, manipulative, forceful, charming, unpredictable, diplomatic, without compromising yourself or others. You can have grown-up fun.

Why you are like this

You are like this because you *want* to be. You have made a choice to interact with people in this way, and are confident enough to take risks and put yourself out there.

Maybe you are one fortunate person who has always had a healthy level of self-esteem and who has never had to fumble for the right thing to say and do. More likely, you have put in some work on yourself and have developed the kind of self-respect that enables effective ways of thinking and behaving.

What you do

Being proactive

You make things happen, and you take chances. This means you can start discussions and conversations, you can change the subject and you can make suggestions. You don't wait for others to take the lead or give you permission to do so.

Signature sentence – How about/What if we/
Can we talk about …

Taking responsibility for your feelings

You don't blame other people for your emotional states. You sometimes feel hurt, angry and resentful, and you feel all the uncomfortable emotions we experience, but you see your emotional response as your reaction to others' words and actions and not as something they have forced on you.

Signature sentence – I felt hurt when you went
behind my back. (Note the difference: you don't say,
'You hurt me by going behind my back.')

Being upfront with people

Your style is to be direct but never confrontational. You don't hide behind someone else, claiming that an unpopular decision is theirs. You don't complain behind people's backs, but say nothing to their face. You don't simmer silently. When there is something you feel you want to say, you find a way of saying it that makes things easy for you and for the other person.

Signature sentence – I'd like to talk about what
happened yesterday.

Judging situations and adjusting your behaviour

This is a skill that illustrates your sensitivity to people. You know that just because you can say something doesn't mean you have to. There are some situations which can be handled with the lightest of touches and some which require the full arsenal of your assertiveness skills and you are able to judge which is which. You can challenge an action or a comment, or you can shrug it off with a smile and a joke if you decide that is the best response. You recognise when something bothers you on a level which requires some action and when something is a minor niggle which you can choose to live with.

Signature sentence – It's not worth us falling out over this.

Moving on when getting it wrong

No one is superhuman. It is OK not to know everything and not to understand everything. It is okay to make mistakes. You make mistakes, mess up and get things wrong but you know you cannot change the past and what is done is done. You can learn from your mistakes and decide to get it right next time.

Being a great communicator

You make strong connections with all the people in your orbit: those with whom you are closest and most intimate;

those in your wider circle of friends and family; your work or play colleagues; those with whom you share a neighbourhood; strangers with whom you cross paths …

As a speaker

You have learnt, and you constantly practise, the knack of saying the right thing. That means that whatever you say, whether you are involved in a deep and meaningful discussion, having a laugh with pals, making a complaint, telling someone off or paying a compliment, you express yourself appropriately and directly in a way which develops and maintains positive relationships.

As a listener

It is not just about getting your point across, it is about listening to other people in an active and totally engaged way. You hear the words and you read between the lines. You are tuned into body language and non-verbal signals. You give responses and ask questions which demonstrate that you are paying attention and which work towards building understanding.

Your voice

Your default tone is calm and level. You vary the way you speak to suit the occasion. When it is required, you can sound firm, apologetic, enthusiastic, playful, decisive, tender or conciliatory. You manage and control the way you speak so that your voice matches the words and the ideas you are conveying. You are not afraid of pauses and you are not afraid of silence.

Your body language
The fact that you are comfortable in your own skin is reflected in your body language, which is relaxed and assured. Your posture is nicely upright, without being stiff on the one hand or apologetic on the other. You judge the appropriate distance to keep so that you neither crowd people nor remain too distant. Your gestures are open and do not present barriers and you manage eye contact effectively.

What you gain

Your life and your relationships become more exciting, more creative and more dynamic as you enter the grown-up world of confident communication and say goodbye to fear, to game-playing and to being scared of taking risks.

You experience less anxiety. Because you actively manage your feelings and your relationships, you aren't scared and you don't have to avoid people and situations. Not for you the hurried dash into the nearest shop to avoid coming face to face with someone you feel awkward with. You don't need to pretend to be out when your mother, your daughter, your ex or the school-run organiser calls. You can choose this tactic but if you do, it is not because you don't know any other way to handle the situation.

What you lose

It will be strange at first, for you and for other people. Even if you have been unhappy with your behaviour patterns, at least they were familiar. If someone is used to you never disagreeing, it will be a shock for him or her to hear you speak up. If you have never asked for anything, a rise, an evening out or a cup of coffee, people may be taken aback when you do. You and others will need to adjust.

But everyone will get used to it. There may be some people who do not like the more upfront, straight-talking, vibrant you. You might be a challenge to them. They'll get over it, and if they don't, are they people whose opinion matters to you? You need not let their problem become yours.

You may need to adjust to not always getting your own way. You might know what you would like, but, as the Rolling Stones sang so plaintively, you can't always get what you want (although, on reflection, Mick and the boys probably did). If you have been used to thinking in terms of who wins and who loses, the switch to thinking instead about solutions and compromises may be something of a wrench. But the short-term pain is far outweighed by the long-term gains.

Leading lady

There are many role models we could choose from the women we encounter in our personal and working lives, from those we observe in public life and from the fictional portrayals which enliven books, songs, stage and screen. You might like to choose your own example or even draw up a list.

Here's a starter suggestion: Dustin Hoffman's character in the film *Tootsie* (1982) who discovers assertiveness when he 'becomes' a woman. His declaration to his romantic interest – 'I was a better man with you as a woman than I ever was with a woman as a man' – is a testament to the life-enhancing attributes of smart girls.

·

CHAPTER THREE

Getting the Right Mindset

At this point you might be thinking that all sounds fine, and yes, I'd like to handle things differently and I'd like to enjoy all the benefits of a more dynamic approach, but I can't because:

+ I'm just not like that.

+ The trouble with me is I'm a soft person.

+ I'm afraid I have to speak up.

+ I'm too nice.

+ I can't help losing my temper when someone riles me.

+ I just can't say no when I think someone needs me.

+ You can't change the way you are, can you?

+ I'm really shy/unconfident/withdrawn/reserved.

✦ I'm just a bossy person – I even made my dolls stand
in silence.

Some of our personality traits are caused by a complex mix
of heredity and environment and are an integral part of
our make-up. This can lead us to think we are the way we
are, for better or worse, and we just have to put up with
it. We slap on a label saying 'quiet' or 'caring', 'self-centred'
or 'insecure' and assume this characteristic is as much an
unchangeable part of us as the size of our feet or the colour
of our eyes.

When we do this, we discount the possibility of change.

But there is so much we can change. Although many
aspects of ourselves do stay the same throughout our lives,
we are not fixed entities, and we can adapt and evolve. We
are not talking complete reinvention here, but about the
small but significant alterations we can make to the way
that we think and the way that we act.

How do you know that you or anyone else is 'shy',
'supportive' or 'a good friend'? Is it because we say so?
Yeah, right, we know how well that one works! The boss
who claims to be approachable as she spits and snarls at
anyone who crosses her path before she has had her caf-
feine fix, or the team mate who talks up her commitment
to the team, then goes for solo glory, or the professed loyal
friend who … no, let's not go there. Too painful! The fact is
that our personality and our attitude are perceived through
the way that we behave, through what we do and what we
say, through how we do it and how we say it.

We do have set patterns of behaviour, and predictable reactions to people and situations. You might be in the habit of being dismissive if someone pays you a compliment or you might always give in to certain people when they make requests you'd rather refuse.

There is one particular person at work who always winds you up. You get nervous and flustered when you have to deal with your child's teacher. You can tell people at work that you are not happy with something, but you keep quiet about it.

These are habits of behaviour. But here is the good news: these habits are not set in stone and, if you want to, you can change them.

Think of your most ingrained patterns of behaviour: a daily or familiar journey, a meal that you rustle up regularly or perhaps your weekly supermarket trawl. You might have experienced getting to the end of the journey and thinking, 'Did I stop at the lights? Did I go round the one-way system?' Yes, you did! As you finish cooking, you cannot actually remember adding all the ingredients, but they are all included. When you unpack the shopping trolley, you cannot recall picking up the butter, but yes, there it is. Your hand went out automatically at the right place. In these situations, you are on autopilot and don't have to consciously think about what you are doing.

Imagine now that the familiar journey has changed: you work somewhere else, friends and family members have moved. Or you are cooking a meal you have never tried before. Or the supermarket layout has been changed. Now you have to think about what you are doing. You won't have to think about it for very long, though.

Sooner than you imagine, the new behaviour becomes a habit. Before you know it, you are making the new journey without giving it a thought, and you could walk round the supermarket aisles blindfold. This is a process that you will experience over and over again.

So you can change the way you behave. You can act in a different way. You can say different words. At first, it will feel strange and unfamiliar, but it will become easier. As with so many things, the first time is the most difficult.

Developing self-esteem

Self-esteem and self-confidence are at the core of assertive behaviour. These qualities are not to do with bigging yourself up or thinking you are more important than anyone else. Rather, they reflect self-knowledge and self-acceptance. Behaving assertively will help you to grow in self-knowledge and self-liking. As we have seen, lack of confidence can lead to behaving like a bulldozer, a push-over or a snake. The kind of confidence we are talking about here is being comfortable in your own skin, being able to acknowledge and celebrate your strengths, and being ready to face and challenge the weaknesses that prevent you from making positive changes in your life.

Significant strengths

What's that? You haven't got any? Oh yes, you have! What 'strength' means in this context is an ability to behave in a way that helps you achieve your goal. It means having attitudes that support your aim, and having a level of knowledge and understanding that enables you to successfully develop different ways of engaging with people.

When you work to one of your strengths, you feel good about yourself. You feel confident and comfortable. Here are ten important strengths that are reflected in assertive behaviour:

- The ability to talk and express feelings

- The ability to listen

- Empathy

- Tolerance

- Flexibility

- Courage

- Respect

- Resilience

- Kindness

- Open-mindedness

It is more than likely that you will have exhibited most if not all of these qualities in different contexts. In your multiple roles, whatever they are, as mother, grandmother, daughter, sister, friend, aunt, cousin, neighbour, work-mate, colleague, acquaintance, employee, boss, whatever, you probably demonstrate, or have demonstrated, these attributes, which are part of the bedrock of assertive be-haviour. Recognise and celebrate the occasions on which you communicate these strengths.

· TAKE THREE ·

Choose one of the above strengths and identify three situations in which you demonstrated it:

- *I accepted that Mick and I have different political views.*

- *I told Charlie I enjoyed her talk.*

- *I listened empathetically when Libby told me all about the exciting development in her life, even though I thought she was mad to even think about giving up her job to go and live in the back of beyond with someone she met last month on the Internet.*

If you have done one of these things, or something simi-lar, you have not only demonstrated strengths which will help you develop assertive behaviour, but you have shown qualities of personality and character that make you valued. Let yourself feel good about them.

Knowing your soft spots

Soft spots, weaknesses, vulnerable areas – these are the characteristics which can make it difficult for you to behave assertively.

Recognise what these qualities are and be particularly alert to situations that tap into them. Just because they have caused you to behave in a certain way in the past does not mean that you have to let them influence your behaviour in the future.

Letting go of old messages

Our heads are crammed with messages we have received throughout our lives. They are so much a part of us that we don't stop to identify or question them.

When we were young, these messages came mostly from the parent and authority figures in our lives. We absorbed teaching and instructions about the kind of behaviour that was expected of us, expressed in terms such as 'You should', 'You shouldn't', 'You must' and 'You mustn't.'

You may have been taught that it is polite to agree with people, that the only way to handle aggression is to give as good as you get, that you should 'never blow your own trumpet', that you shouldn't be pushy or that you should always put others' needs first. So being a smart cookie, to gain approval and stay out of trouble, you adapted your behaviour accordingly and gave the people in charge what they wanted. You kept quiet rather than disagree, you didn't ask for anything in case it drew attention to you. Or you played up, stamping your little foot and sulking and threatening like Violet Elizabeth Bott in the *Just William* books: 'I'll thcream and thcream and thcream 'till I'm thick.'

Trouble is, it is not so smart to hang on to these ideas if they are not working for you and if they are preventing you from functioning and communicating as the fully real-ised grown-up girl that you are. If an old message is play-ing in your head and getting in the way of you behaving confidently and appropriately, you can decide to turn it off. You can replace it with a message that supports you rather than stifles you.

As for those of us who hear ourselves using admoni-tory proverbs and phrases our mothers or grandmothers used because they heard their mothers or grandmothers use them – 'Waste not want not,' 'Don't care was made to care,' 'Handsome is as handsome does' – it is a short step to stockpiling tins of corned beef and collecting pieces of string too short to use. As that master of the witty one- or two-liner, Oscar Wilde, said, 'All women become like their mothers. That is their tragedy.' But then he added, 'No man does. That is his.'

Yes, mothers rock. Be the one you choose to be, if appro-priate, and honour your own mama for the good things she gave you. Ditch the unhelpful things.

It is time to let go. Time to move on. We have all done it in our lives.

· TAKE THREE ·

Think of three 'messages' that play in your head and prevent you from behaving assertively. Replace each one with a more helpful thought.

For example, if the message which makes you say yes to every request that comes your way is 'It's wrong to be selfish,' you could think instead, 'It's not selfish to think about requests and how they affect my time and my life. It's actually OK and grown-up.'

Taking responsibility for yourself

This really is the light bulb moment. Accepting responsibility for your own actions, thoughts and emotions is at the core of being a smart girl.

As soon as you begin to do this, you will feel more comfortable, more together and more in control. Instead of thinking that other people and circumstances make you feel and behave in certain ways, you take ownership of your feelings and responses.

This makes you feel tall in a way that the steepest,

sassiest, sexiest stilettos produced by Manolo, Jimmy Choo and the gang never could. You gain inner strength and calmness (a great base from which to engage with others), and a wonderful bonus is an increase in understanding and compassion.

The guilt hook

Guilt is an uncomfortable and painful state to be in. Legal, social and religious structures are based on notions of guilt and wrongdoing, with agreed and understood penalties for breaking rules and the law. The awareness that we have done wrong, have committed a crime, have hurt people, have behaved in a way which rightly incurs blame and deserves punishment is difficult to live with.

Why waste another precious second feeling guilty about things that are not crimes? About things that are not even wrong, except in our own heads? If you count up all the minutes we waste feeling 'guilty' about things that are not crimes, you could be looking at the whole of a lifetime.

We scatter the word 'guilty' like confetti at a wedding. We misapply it to a range of situations. Sometimes we use it to paint ourselves in a good light: we are so nice that we suffer when we think we hurt others, and we care so much about what others think that we beat ourselves up when we make choices that some imaginary person will disapprove of. We are revealing ourselves as needy and overanxious to please. We are not 'guilty', we are self-absorbed.

Getting rid of the guilt

Look at each of the following situations in a different way. Instead of being caught by the guilt hook, think clearly about the issues involved and the real nature of your feelings.

PICTURE THIS

Your friend wants you to go sales shopping with her, and you don't want to.

Guilt alert!

TRY THIS

Tell yourself you are only saying no to going shopping: you are not committing a crime. You are not rejecting your friend: you are making a choice about an activity. And what would be the consequences if you went along reluctantly? You would feel resentful and put upon. And how would your friend feel if she knew? She may well feel equally resentful at being placed in this position.

Your guilt at saying no is totally misplaced. The only crime you have committed is a crime against friendship. Your assumption that your friend could not handle your rejection of the request actually belittles her.

PICTURE THIS

You are trying to lose weight to fit into your beach outfit. You eat some chocolate.

Call the guilt police!

TRY THIS

Don't use the word 'guilt'. So you dropped off your self-imposed diet wagon for a moment. You may be disappointed in yourself, you may be demotivated or you may experience a number of emotions, but guilt should not be one of them.

PICTURE THIS

You have planned to spend the afternoon clearing out the garage and you start to watch an old film on television and can't drag yourself away.

Guilty as charged!

TRY THIS

Where exactly is the crime here? You decided to take on a task, and then you changed your mind. That is your choice. It might be that this kind of thing frequently happens and you rarely complete what you set out to do. If it worries you, you could give some thought about why this may be. But don't blame yourself. Anyway, some old films demand to be watched, don't they?! A household task versus a steamy Douglas Sirk? No contest, we say!

PICTURE THIS

Your colleague works late to get an urgent task finished and you leave punctually because you have an appointment.

Time for a latte and a guilt sandwich!

TRY THIS

You are responsible for your actions, and other people are responsible for theirs. You can negotiate this and similar situations with your work mates in a grown-up way. Bleating (openly or silently) about how guilty you feel is demeaning to you both.

PICTURE THIS

You are angry with someone and they burst into tears.

How can you live with the guilt!

TRY THIS

You may be upset because you don't like to see the other person upset. You may feel that you want to consider if you were too strong or unfair in what you said. Depending on the circumstances, you might feel regret or you might feel your words or actions were justified. Whatever the case, don't let someone's tears become your guilt hook.

Guilt is a burden. If you have to carry it, it is a hard row to hoe. But don't, please don't, manufacture your own burden and let it weigh you down.

The blame game

When you blame someone for your emotional state, you give them power over you. You relinquish ownership of your own being and allow another person to shape and control events and your reactions to them.

It can be a knee-jerk reaction, a hangover from playground days when our automatic response when we got into trouble was to say, 'So-and-so made me!' This is echoed in the present day when we say things like 'She makes me so angry' and 'Did you see that Danny made Ellie cry?' We don't realise we are turning ourselves into powerless victims and what is even worse is the people to whom we give this power are often those we do not like or respect.

Constantly blaming other people is unrealistic and dishonest. When you refuse to take any personal responsibility for decisions or events, you make sure that you cannot be criticised if things go wrong.

It is also a waste of time, because the energy you spend blaming others for what goes wrong could be put to better use looking for solutions and ways out.

Setting goals for new behaviour

Deciding to 'behave more assertively' is a great start, but it is too sweeping a resolution to be of much practical use. You will find it helpful to narrow down this idea so that you focus on specific patterns of behaviour that you intend to develop.

When you identify these patterns, phrase them in positive, specific terms. If you think in terms of what you will stop doing, all you will hear in your head will be the very thing you want to eliminate. 'Don't think of Lady Gaga' – what did you just think of? Right. The same thing will happen if you think 'I'm going to be less shy' or 'I'm going to stop agreeing with everything'. The words 'shy' and 'agreeing' will be there, haunting and taunting you. In addition, if you repeat to yourself the words 'mustn't' and 'shouldn't', you will swamp yourself in negativity.

A positive picture

Having a positive goal and a positive image of yourself in the new situation is inspiring and motivating. Visualise yourself in your new role. See yourself as the person who behaves in this new way and imagine how good it will feel.

Baby steps

Set yourself a small, achievable goal. A tiny change can have a huge impact. If you try to do too much at once, or take on too daunting a situation, the chances are that you will feel discouraged and give up. Deciding that from tomorrow you will be the life and soul of every social gathering when today you never open your mouth is not going to work.

PICTURE THIS
You would like to be able to be more outgoing.

TRY THIS
Say hello to someone you see every day but have never greeted.

Say hello to someone while you are waiting at a bus stop.

PICTURE THIS

You would like to make requests.

TRY THIS

Ask someone who is going to the drinks machine to get a cappuccino for you as well.

· **TAKE THREE** ·

Think of three situations in which you would like to behave more assertively. For each, identify one small step that you can take immediately.

·

CHAPTER FOUR

Step-by-step Guide to Assertive Communication

Once you get the hang of it, it is as easy as 1-2-3 – just make that 3 a 6 to do a really good job …

STEP 1 Identify what you are feeling

The first thing you need to do is to work out exactly what you are feeling – and this is not as easy as it sounds. In challenging encounters – that is, encounters, events, conversations and actions that challenge our sense of well-being and equilibrium – our first response is often physical.

Someone says something and your eyes fill with tears, or your heart thumps and your hands go into fists. Or you may find yourself smiling in a fixed kind of way because the genuine smile just doesn't come. If you like what you see or hear, your voice might rise and your tone become enthusiastic. You might get butterflies in your stomach.

In some situations, you may find yourself automatically mirroring the other person's physical state, smiling or frowning because that is what they are doing.

Your body's reaction is a guide to your emotional response. Learn to read the signs and identify what you feel, for example, when you are not invited to a social event, when you find out that your child is being bullied, when your friend gets the promotion that you wanted or when a suggestion you make is turned down.

You need to nail the feeling with a word or phrase that accurately describes your response. You may be in the habit of using just a few words to cover a whole range of feelings. Every positive experience might be 'nice', and every negative one 'rubbish'. You might be 'fed up' about everything from losing your umbrella to losing your phone to losing your job. This makes it difficult for others to recognise and understand the nature and intensity of your feelings, and lessens the assertive impact of your communication.

Some words you might use:

angry	envious	delighted	rejected
furious	rebuffed	elated	embarrassed
upset	resentful	overwhelmed	uncertain
annoyed	nervous	anxious	celebratory
irritated	intimidated	thrilled	intrigued
frustrated	daunted	excited	interested
humiliated	protective	gratified	energised
put down	let down	unsettled	
jealous	pleased	disturbed	

· TAKE THREE ·

In the coming week, choose three occasions on which you feel a strong response to someone's actions or words or an event. Find the right word or phrase to describe your feelings.

You could identify just how you feel after the following:

- a social event

- a parents' consultation

- a difficult day

- watching a film you enjoyed

- watching a film you didn't enjoy

- a disagreement

- seeing your friend's new romance with someone else

- receiving an invitation

- being criticised for something

- someone close to you is unhappy

- receiving a compliment; someone rejects your advice about a problem

STEP 2 Identify your motives for communicating assertively

Think about what kind of communication you are initiating. You might want to let someone know that his or her behaviour has hurt you, pleased you or inconvenienced you. You might want to ask someone to stop or to start behaving in a certain way. Perhaps you would like to discuss something, or ask or give advice. Maybe you want to make a suggestion, start a discussion, be entertaining or explain your reasons for something you have done or said.

STEP 3 Make an 'I' statement

When you express your feelings, your statement should begin with the word 'I' or 'My'. Not because you are the most important person in the universe, but because it is crucial that you accept and acknowledge your own feelings.

So it is not 'You're so selfish' and 'You made me angry', it is 'I feel', 'I think', 'My take on this is' and 'In my opinion'.

Now this might be quite a step for some people – yes, Ms Pushover, we are talking to you in particular – because there may be a few old messages running through your head about it being self-centred to talk about yourself and that the 'I' word is a bit rude. Wrong message! It is good and it is smart to take responsibility for your feelings, and expressing them directly makes your communication stronger and more compelling.

Hear the difference:

+ *It's annoying.*

+ I'm annoyed.

+ *That's a good colour on you.*

+ I really like that colour on you.

+ *It was hurtful of you to forget my birthday.*

+ I am hurt that you forgot my birthday.

· TAKE THREE ·

Choose to make three 'I' statements every day.
They can be about little things.

Instead of 'It's hot in here', say, 'I'm a bit hot –
okay if I open the window?'

STEP 4 Acknowledge the other person

Of course, it is not all about you, no matter how strongly
you feel about something or how wrong you think someone else is. Show you understand, accept or empathise
with another person's position. This doesn't necessarily

mean you agree with them. It means you show respect for their right to their own thoughts and feelings, just as you show respect to yours. Your statement of acknowledgement could begin with phrases such as:

✦ *I understand that you …*

✦ *I realise that …*

STEP 5 Communicate the point you want to make

This is where you say, if appropriate, what you want, need or would like to happen, as you identified in Step 2. You should make clear what this is, whether it is something you would like someone else to start or stop doing, or something you would like to discuss, something you want to get off your chest or something you want to share.

STEP 6 Listen and discuss

Unless it really is an 'end of' situation, make it clear that you want to hear someone's reaction and show that you are ready to listen and, if appropriate, negotiate.

Use this structure as a framework for all your assertive communication.

This could be you

PICTURE THIS

You receive a compliment about a flyer you produced for a local event and thanked the person warmly.

You sent an email to someone whose literature course you recently attended, telling him or her that you found it enjoyable and inspirational.

You apologised to your child for not trusting him or her to keep the house rules about sleepovers.

You told the restaurant manager that you thought coffee on the house would be a welcome gesture to compensate for the sub-standard quality of the meal you just had.

You told your work colleague you would not be able to complete a project in the given time and asked for a later deadline.

You told the person who supported you through a bout of illness how much you appreciated all that they did.

You told someone you loved him or her.

Look at you! You have handled a range of challenging situations confidently and gracefully, and made life better for yourself and for those who share your life. All you need to behave like this is a little know-how.

Useful techniques

How to judge situations

Just because you can do something, it doesn't mean you have to. Many a veteran sister of the sexual revolution came to this realisation late in life.

You don't have to meet every challenging situation with a full-on assertive response. Life would be a bit heavy if you did. There are some things you can ignore or brush aside.

Some situations are best handled with humour. Tune into your inner light-hearted child and choose to make a joke, to tease someone or to do some mock self-deprecation – yes, that's me, isn't it, always ready with the wrong answer, ha ha (just be sure you are only playing and not really putting yourself down).

There may be some issues you want to park for now, to put in a box to be acted on at a later date, if necessary. On some occasions, you may decide to try a soft-touch approach at first and deliver a stronger response if this doesn't work. The trick is in identifying the best response for each situation.

How much does it bother you?

Step back from the situation and assess, let's say on a scale of 1–10, how much it bothers you. If it is a mild niggle, you might rate it at 1 or 2. If it is something that really bugs you, that never leaves you, that keeps you awake at night or that keeps coming back, then we are talking a 10 or even off the scale.

You might notice the strength of your response doesn't reflect the magnitude of the situation. Something minor can get under your skin, and not in the good way that Cole Porter wrote about – check out Frank Sinatra's version on *Songs for Swinging Lovers* for the ultimate experience, although many wonderful others have done good jobs – while something that may seem significant to others bounces off you completely.

Don't just think about negative situations: you can be equally disturbed by the awareness that there is something positive you feel you want to do, but haven't had the courage to put into practice.

This could be expressing gratitude to a parent for having supported you through a difficult time. It could be giving an invitation such as asking someone out for a drink or a meal.

How much will it bother you in the future?

Consider the investment you are making, in terms of challenge, engagement or follow-up, and decide how much this situation will matter in a week's, in a month's, in a year's time.

Balance this against the level of intensity of feeling and the effort it would take to tackle this issue. If you know that it will still matter, and that it is likely you will regret not taking action, then resolve to do it.

Is anyone else affected?

Something might not bother you personally, but might matter to a person for whom you have some responsibility, either personally or professionally. You might laugh off a colleague's cutting remarks, but team members might be upset by them. If you need to, use the previous two processes to assess the kind of intervention that would be appropriate.

What will be gained?

Decide what will be achieved if you take on a particular issue and balance this consideration against the others. If you need to put in a lot of emotional and practical effort for very little outcome, you might decide that this is something you can live with or treat lightly. On the other hand, lots of little gains can make you and the other people in your life feel sooo good …

· TAKE THREE ·

Choose three situations you feel you need to deal with. Give each one a mark on the 1–10 scale. If any are above 5, decide what you are going to do about it. (Ignoring it is not an option!)

How to hold your ground

There will be occasions when your ability to be assertive is challenged by the other person's arguments and you feel your self-confidence being undermined.

A strategy that is helpful in these circumstances is to repeat the core phrase of your message, bypassing attempts to talk you down or talk you out of it.

This is sometimes referred to as the 'stuck record' strategy, a historical reference that recalls a time when, yes, astonishing as it may seem to those of you with more recent birth certificates, music came in the form of a quaint grooved vinyl disc. Now listen carefully. You would place this disc on a turntable, and carefully, very carefully, you would lower a needle (also known as a stylus) onto the first groove. A hiss, a crackle, then would issue forth the most wonderful sounds you'd ever heard in your life. The experience was somehow only intensified by the way the needle would sometimes get stuck in a groove so that the phrase on which it paused would be repeated over and over again.

The 'stuck record' technique works when someone is being persistent. The principle is that you briefly acknowledge what they are saying, but repeat your core phrase calmly and persistently. This works very well when your request, refusal or observation is clear and unambiguous, and when you are not prepared to negotiate or compromise.

PICTURE THIS

You need your son to pick you up from your evening class. He would rather you made any other arrangement as long as it does not inconvenience him.

TRY THIS

'I know you and Mandy will be watching a DVD tonight, but I do need you to pick me up.'

'Yes, I could walk home, but I want you to pick me up.'

How to avoid getting sucked in

Use the table tennis bat

Can you see yourself, bat in hand, with the little ball bouncing towards you?! The little ball is a bundle of words that someone is sending your way to distract you from what you are trying to say. You want the kids to tidy the living room before your mother arrives. One of them says they need to get on with homework, and you find yourself in the middle of an argument about who has most homework to do and whose is most important, and the living room is still in a mess …

You want to know when your sofa-surfing friend is going to move on, and he or she keeps saying how much they appreciate you putting them up and what an understanding friend you are, and there you are, yet again, discussing their problematic relationship and no nearer to knowing when they will be leaving …

Imagine yourself, in the calmest possible way, batting the words to one side, so that they are no longer in your way. You do this with a little phrase that acknowledges, but doesn't pick up or respond to what has been said:

✦ *'That may be the case, but I need you to tidy the room now.'*

✦ *'That's great to hear, but I need to know exactly when you are moving back to your own place.'*

It is helpful not to make any specific reference to their words, because if you do, you open the door that leads you in.

How to defuse a situation

Agree

This can take the wind out of someone's sails, particularly if you feel you are being goaded. It is also helpful in situations that you just cannot be bothered to take on. When you say something like 'You could be right about that' or 'You know what? I agree', there is nowhere for the other person to go. It is a great way of feeling calm and in control, because you are choosing not to become involved, and you have set up a barrier that protects you from further discussion.

✦ *'You were really rude to Lynn just now.'*

✦ *'Yes, I think I might have been.'*

✦ *'I can't believe you didn't clear away the dirty glasses.'*

✦ *'I'm a real slob, aren't I.'*

You could use this 'protection time' to think about the comment and decide if you want to take it further. This works if the criticism focuses on a point that might be significant in the relationship.

CHAPTER FIVE

·

How to Say It –
Smart Body Language

Sᴍᴀʀᴛ ʙᴏᴅʏ language should match and reinforce the verbal message that is being delivered. If it doesn't, you send mixed messages and confuse the listener who senses the mismatch between what you say, and how you say it, and loses confidence in you and your conversation.

Even worse, if there is this contradiction between your words and your style of delivery, it is the way you say the words that makes the dominant impression.

PICTURE THIS

Your shoulders are hunched and your eyes are glaring. Your fists are clenched and your jaw is tight. The words shoot out of your mouth like a bullet from a gun: 'I'm not angry!' You bang the table as you speak.

How likely is it that your hapless listener or listeners turn to each other and say, 'That's OK then. She said she wasn't angry'? Yes, about as likely as Dolly Parton letting nature take its course. (It's a great look, Dolly, you clever girl. We love you.)

In fact, those were your actual words, but everything else about your message said the very opposite. Your words were clear but your body language was much stronger and swept them away.

You say, 'I'm sorry.' As you speak, you raise your eyebrows and twist your mouth, and you pronounce the word 'sorr-eee'. Not much of an apology, is it? This response is a challenge to keep on arguing as your body language practically invites the other person to remark that you don't sound very sorry ... perhaps that is what you intended, you manipulative minx! Or perhaps you felt embarrassed and awkward about apologising and managed to get the words out, but detracted from their sincerity by your inappropriate tone and facial expression.

How to get it right

Tone of voice

It has happened to us all. You mean to sound decisive, and your voice comes out aggressive. You want to be firm, but your voice wobbles. You mean to make a joke but your voice gives a sarcastic tone to your words.

It is all about control, and control starts with breathing. Good breathing has a steadying and calming effect, and taking a few deep breaths before you speak is an excellent way to deal with tension and anxiety.

TRY THIS

Take a deep breath from way down in your diaphragm and feel it travel up through your body. Your stomach area is the only part that should move as you do this; if your chest rises and falls, you are breathing too shallowly and that is likely to make you sound weak and fluttery.

Hold the breath for a few seconds, then breathe out very slowly, making sure that all the air is expelled from your lungs. Doing this once or twice will steady you and give you the calm confidence to project your voice appropriately.

Volume

Control the volume of your voice. On occasions when you want your voice to express firmness, forcefulness or anger, you should raise the volume slightly, not so that you are shouting, but to give emphasis to your words.

TRY THIS

Imagine your voice on a scale of 1–10, with 1 being a whisper and 10 being a shout. Read out this sentence beginning at volume level 1 and moving up to 10. Now go back and focus on the middle range, say, between 4 and 7. This should be a comfortable volume for everyday communication, with 6 and 7 being effective for strongly assertive communication. When you want to raise your voice for effect, hear that middle range inside your head and pitch your voice accordingly.

If you speak more loudly than this, you may be perceived as being aggressive, and if you drop down to level 2 or 3, unless you are deliberately doing this for effect, you may come across as timid and uncertain.

Pace

When we are anxious and worked up, we tend to speak too quickly. An average rate of speaking is between 150 and 164 words per minute. If you go above this rate, you will sound nervous and gabbly, and if you go much below it, you will lose people's attention as they start to drop off to sleep.

Speaking slowly can add weight and importance to what you say, but only if this pace is balanced by more rapid delivery. Variety of pace is one of the keys to gaining and keeping the attention of the person you are speaking to.

Inflection

Your voice goes up and down as you speak and changes with the different ideas and emotions you express. When you are excited or nervous, the resonance of your voice comes from high up around your face area, and this results in a high-pitched voice. When your voice resonates lower down in your chest, it emerges with a more serious, con-sidered tone. What is your own pattern of inflection like?

Upspeak

You may in the habit of raising your voice at the end of sentences. Stephen Fry (big respect to his big brain) calls this the 'Australian Question Intonation,' referring to what may or may not be the habit's place of origin. When you want to sound authoritative and to be taken seriously, this intonation does not work. When the pitch of your voice turns every statement into a question, you come across as timid and tentative, as if you are asking your listener for reassurance. You sound nervous and uncertain.

This inflection would be helpful for:

✦ asking a question

✦ encouraging the other person to nod at whatever you say

✦ establishing rapport with someone who speaks like this.

Levelspeak

When your voice is level, and your sentence starts and ends on the same note, it sounds neutral. You are making a statement, not asking a question or giving an order.

This inflection would be helpful for most assertive encounters, including:

✦ opening a discussion

✦ expressing a preference

+ making a request

+ expressing a view

+ giving feedback.

Downspeak

When your voice goes down at the end of your sentence, you make an impact. Your tone adds weight and authority to your words. So, on the occasions when you want to make a strong declaration, let your voice travel through an arc that rises throughout the sentence and drops back down at the end.

This inflection would be helpful for:

+ being emphatic

+ indicating a strong feeling

+ bringing a discussion to an end.

TRY THIS

Say the following sentences in each of the three ways described and notice the different effect of each type of intonation.

'I think we should arrange the meeting for tomorrow morning.'

'I would like a refund.'

'I need to cancel the appointment.'

Posture

Weren't we told to stand up straight, to stop slouching and keep our heads up, and didn't we hate it, when we wanted to protect our budding bodies and our patchy complexions from outside scrutiny? Oh, the acne years … Time to move on! The way you stand, sit and hold yourself makes an impact on the message you are giving and affects your communication. Choose from a range of postures you can adopt to suit different contexts. The important thing is to make sure that the signals your body gives match your intention.

Standing can give you confidence and assurance. A nicely upright posture, not stiff and not slouchy, creates an assertive impression and makes you feel and appear equal to the situation.

Keep your head up, and if you tilt it to one side, be sure this indicates interest and listening and doesn't make you look coy or submissive (whatever you do, don't bat your eyelashes).

If the conversation is one about which you feel nervous, make a particular effort not to fold your arms or cross them across your body, it is a posture that makes you seem ill at ease and defensive. The hugging-yourself look just screams insecurity.

Distribute your weight evenly and avoid the one-hip-jutting-out stance. Keep your body oriented towards the listener and maintain an appropriate distance.

If the other person stands or moves too close, shift your

position and move backwards or to the side. They may not be deliberately crowding your space, but don't allow it to happen.

Similarly, if you find that the distance between you is too great to speak easily, move forward a little and, at the same time, change the angle of your position so you are not seen to be moving in on them.

This posture would be helpful in situations such as:

+ non-social workplace conversations

+ making a complaint about poor service or goods

+ making a firm refusal

+ making a firm request

+ responding to a firm request

+ responding to a critical comment.

Standing is good when the other person is also standing. If you stand and they sit, you can seem overbearing and dominant. If you sit and they stand, you put yourself in a submissive position.

When you are sitting, apply the same rules about keeping your body open. In formal situations such as interviews or professional discussions sit in a comfortably upright and alert position and keep your arms away from your body.

This is particularly important if you cross your legs, which is hard not to do, but if you have legs crossed, plus arms folded or draped across your front, you might as well just scream, 'I don't want to be here! I don't like this! I don't like you!' And if you hook your ankles round the rung of your chair, you look as tense as a stretched rubber band.

It might be just that you feel comfortable with your arms and legs in these positions, but it is always best to assume other people will not give you the benefit of the doubt when they interpret your body language.

Whether you are sitting or standing, be aware of other people's posture and of how closely or not your positions mirror those of the others. Communication will be more effective if you are in broadly similar positions. Don't perch on the edge of your chair if the other person is sitting well back, don't lean against a door if the other person isn't. Keep the direction of your limbs and your trunk in a similar line.

PICTURE THIS

You want to tell a young family member how you feel about him borrowing your car without permission. He is sprawled full length on the sofa.

If you are standing as you begin the conversation, you position yourself as the one who is doing the telling off and him as the one who is on the receiving end. It will be difficult for your communication to develop beyond this. If you sprawl out in the same posture as his, it will be hard to sound firm. Try something in between: sit down near him, but retain an upright posture.

Keep your limbs relaxed. Lean slightly towards him as you speak. Make your gestures expansive, with your hands quite high above your waist. It is likely that your combination of words and body language will encourage him to shift into a slightly more upright position and it will be easier for you to engage in assertive communication.

Space

When you want to make your presence felt, claim some space. Not in a messy, all-over-the-place kind of way but in a way which asserts your status. Without encroaching on anyone else, spread out appropriate belongings such as laptop, notebook, pens, water glass and sit up straight.

Gestures

Without realising it, your hands may be sending non-verbal signals that undermine your words. You may sound confident but if you constantly twiddle your hair, or fiddle with your jewellery or clothing, you will appear nervous and unsure. If your fingers are tightly laced together, you will appear tense, in spite of your attempts to sound relaxed and at ease. Habits such as drumming the table with your fingertips or swinging a leg to and fro as you speak suggest you are feeling stressed.

Over-expansive hand gestures can be distracting. If you compulsively mime every word you speak, drawing in the air to show what you mean by 'ticket', 'book' or 'list' and making huge circles to indicate concepts such a 'big' or 'a lot', you make it harder for your listener to take in what you are saying.

However, if you use your hands effectively, they can support your words and help you appear more confident and assertive.

When you are communicating a decision or making a definitive statement, a gesture such as one where you bring your parallel hands down sharply, in a kind of chopping style, emphasises your resolve. Use this gesture with the 'downspeak' intonation and you will sound authoritative and assured.

Palms up

Keep your palms open as much as possible, particularly when you want to convince someone of your sincerity. Traditionally, this gesture is associated with openness and honesty as it shows you are not carrying a weapon and do not present a threat.

Extending your hands with the palms up is an inclusive gesture that indicates your willingness to listen and cooperate. You probably do this instinctively in certain situations, but when we feel nervous or under pressure, we are likely to clench our fists or lace our fingers together in a tight knot. Relax your fingers and keep them spread out.

Palms down

Palms down is a helpful gesture in some circumstances. If you want to come across really strongly, hold your hands just above waist height, with the palms down. This gesture might accompany a strong order or request to do something, just do it, please. You might depress your hands as you speak for added emphasis.

If, on the other hand, your words are suggesting harmony, you can underline this feeling by putting your hands in front of you at waist height and spreading them out, palms down, in a movement that suggests soothing and smoothing. This gesture might accompany a reassuring statement such as 'I think that together we can sort this out'. You will give the impression of calm, unruffled control.

TRY THIS

Take the sentence:

'So I need it done by Thursday at the latest.'

Say it with the chopping gesture and the downspeak intonation.

How do you sound? Is anyone going to argue? You are having the final word, girl, and you are giving it without shouting or pleading, in a nicely authoritative way.

Now say it with the smoothing gesture and the level intonation.

How do you sound? Much softer, probably. Much more gentle and conciliatory. Much more bringing people on board.

You choose – just make your voice and your gestures match your words and the message you are conveying.

Facial expression

You feel you are assertive, approachable, upfront but your face might be saying something else entirely. You may be in the habit of frowning all the time, with just that little furrow between the eyes that tells the world not only are you unafraid of wrinkles but that you are busy and preoccupied and don't want to be addressed.

You might have the kind of expression that makes others tell you to cheer up (totally infuriating, we know) and you say you can't help it, it's just the way you look.

There might be some physical aspects that you cannot alter, but many people who permanently have an expression like a smacked bottom could make a few changes that would dramatically alter the impression they make.

Public face

You will be perceived as communicative and approachable if your expression is alert and engaged.

TRY THIS

Imagine you catch an unexpected glimpse of a friend in the distance, someone you are pleased to see. What happens to your face? You probably find that your eyebrows go up just a little, your eyes widen just a trifle, and your mouth turns up just a tiny bit.

That is a good look to take out in public. Slap it on as if it were a favourite lipstick. You will feel confident and assertive and are likely to be perceived as such.

Range of expressions

Smiles are great! They make you feel good, and they make other people feel good as well. Smiles get a positive response – when they appear in the right way and the right place.

It is unassertive to smile too much. This is what we do when we are nervous, guilty or angry. Even if our words carry a clear message, we undermine it with facial expressions that suggest that we want to diminish the importance and take the sting out of what we say. 'Please still like me,' our smile says. 'I'm not being horrible, honest. I don't really mean it.'

Let your face express the emotions you feel. Smile when you are amused, happy, pleased, engaged, understanding, joking … When you are speaking seriously or sternly, keep your facial expression steady and open and do not smile.

Frown when you are less than pleased, raise your eyebrows when you are surprised, look puzzled when you don't understand. You might think that masking your feelings with a blank expression is good self-control, but it may be seen as an aggressive tactic. When your expression and your words match and reinforce each other, your communication is open, straightforward and has impact.

Eye contact

You cannot behave assertively without making appropriate eye contact. If you glare, you will be seen as threatening; if you refuse to meet someone's gaze, you will be seen as shifty and untrustworthy. These are false impressions but undoing a misleading impression is hard work. It is better to develop a confident use of eye contact and get your point across effectively.

When you are speaking, it is usual not to maintain a steady gaze. You will make brief eye contact, look away for moment or two, then make contact again. If you are speaking to a group of people, make fleeting eye contact with them all and 'collect' their gazes.

Be careful not to make contact with just one of the group, something you might be tempted to do if there is an obvious 'leader' such as the main interviewer or the most senior person. (If there is one person in whom you have particular interest that you want to signal, eye contact is a good way to do it.) It is different when you are listening, as you then have a choice.

You could keep eye contact for about 80 per cent of the time and look away when the speaker looks away. This does give your eyes a rest and prevents you from going into 'staring' mode but you run the risk of not synchronising with the speaker and seeming a bit startled and shifty when you look back.

It may be safer to maintain steady eye contact (after all, in everyday situations it is not often that someone speaks at great length without interruption) and when you feel your gaze becoming fixed and your eyes growing tired, shift the focus.

See the person's face as a triangle, with the forehead at the top narrowing down to the chin. Your eyes can move within that space. A safe place for them to go is the bridge of the nose. It looks like eye contact, but it is an easy gaze to manage.

If you want to keep matters business-like and professional, keep to the top half within the triangle. In more social situations, you can move your gaze further down the facial triangle to the area between the eyes and the mouth.

Be careful not to be seen lingering too long on someone's rather big nose, unfortunate spot or their mouth.

Reading body language

Assertive communication involves being constantly aware of other people's feelings and reactions. Their non-verbal signals will tell you as much, if not more, than their words, so as you talk, tune in to the whole message.

Beware of over-interpreting what you see and of jumping to conclusions based on one or two observations.

If someone seems to be avoiding eye contact, don't assume they are trying to hide something or they can't be trusted. It could be the person is shy or anxious and lacks confidence. It is also possible that unlike you, they haven't learnt the skills of managing eye contact. Their lack of eye contact could also reflect different cultural norms.

Similarly, people cross their arms for all kinds of reasons – feeling a bit chilly, trying to hide where a button has dropped off, trying to hide a curry stain that didn't come out, copying the person they are speaking to – anything other than feeling defensive.

TRY THIS

Look for three pieces of evidence to back up each example of non-verbal communication. These could include:

+ spoken words that support or contradict what you have observed

+ other non-verbal messages that support or contradict what you have observed

+ the duration of the signal

+ the physical context.

How to use what you observe

You can choose to ignore what you perceive. If someone verbally agrees to do something but their posture and facial expression tell you they are unhappy about it, you don't have to indicate you realise this. It might suit you to accept the agreement without comment.

For example, if you are referring to agreed house rules for young family people, about time spent on the Internet, say, or school night activities, you might decide not to respond to non-verbal messages that suggest you are being a totally unreasonable fascist for asking that the rules should be kept. You can refuse to rise to the bait and just ignore them.

In other situations, you might choose to show you recognise negative feelings. You could say something like:

✦ *'You seem unhappy with that?'* (An upspeak intonation works here.)

✦ *'I get the feeling that you're not entirely on board with this.'*

✦ *'Would you like to discuss this further?'*

✦ *'Should we talk a little more about this?'*

✦ *'I know you've said it's okay, but I'm getting a very negative vibe.'*

Then, depending on the reply, it is your decision whether or not to pursue the matter.

This practice is a good way of flushing out manipulative behaviour. Your assertive response puts the encounter on an open footing and gives the other person an opportunity to disclose their real feelings.

·

CHAPTER SIX

Saying No Without Losing Your Family, Friends or Your Job

Why it is so hard to say no

It should be straightforward. Someone asks you to do something, you don't want to do it, and you say so. Simple. Oh, if only! What really happens is that we get bogged down with anxieties about the consequences of our refusal and enter a bizarre world if we believe that our saying no to anything will lead to disaster in our personal and professional lives.

We imagine that unless we agree to everything we are asked, we will end up as lonely bag ladies with only a cat for company, and even the cat might desert us if we say no to its constant mewing for titbits …

Some of the reasons for saying yes when we want to say no:

✦ You think that the person asking will be offended by a refusal.

✦ You think that your professional standing will be damaged.

✦ You think that you will not be seen as a team player.

✦ You think that you will be seen as selfish.

✦ You think that your refusal will be held against you.

✦ You are a bit in awe of the person who is asking.

✦ You really like the person who is asking.

✦ You are scared of the person who is asking.

✦ You don't want to be the only one who is refusing.

✦ You think that if you refuse something, you will always be refused in turn.

We often guess what the consequence is likely to be, assume the worst and give a reply based on faulty thinking, falling once again into the trap of taking on responsibility for other people's feelings (not to mention taking on our favourite clairvoyant role in which we just know without being told what people are thinking).

This pattern of thought and behaviour plunges you into a damaging way of life in which you suffer the consequences of saying 'yes' all the time:

+ You feel tired and put-upon.

+ You sometimes suspect you are taken for granted.

+ You feel overloaded.

+ You don't get the things done that you want to do.

+ You feel out of control of your time.

+ You feel out of control in your relationships.

+ Your stress levels rise.

+ You feel resentful of people who ask you to do things.

+ You don't always deliver what you promise.

+ You don't always see things through.

+ You are always under pressure.

+ Your presence and impact are diluted.

+ Your real desires, passions and commitments are invisible.

The head stuff

A change of mindset is required here. Replace the attitude that you just cannot say no with the perception that you can, you really can. Take on board the idea that the ability to say no when appropriate says wonderful things about you. Far from being perceived as a nasty, no-can-do, no-friends person, people will see this:

+ Someone who can be trusted

+ Someone who takes people and requests seriously

+ Someone who has a professional approach to time management

+ Someone who is efficient and effective

+ Someone who thinks about the consequences of actions

+ Someone with self-respect

+ Someone who respects others

+ Someone with a good work-life balance

That someone could be *you*.

Gracious ways of saying no

You don't have to be gracious but it is much nicer if you can be. 'No' needn't be the abrupt bark the word may suggest. If you need it to sound this way, in extreme situations, have the word ready and spit it out. Don't be scared of giving a forceful, no-holds-barred, back-off refusal if that is what the situation requires.

Many of the circumstances you would like to handle more confidently, though, aren't extreme; they are the day-to-day requests and expectations you find difficult to refuse or to negotiate. There are ways of not saying 'yes' which get your point across firmly so you feel nicely confident and in control and demonstrate respect and understanding of the other person.

The power of the pause

Giving an immediate reply can be a recipe for disaster. There are all kinds of reasons why we rush in with an ill-advised 'yes' – we're in a hurry, the other person is in a hurry, we want to get them off the phone, it's easier to shut them up and sort it out later (no, it isn't, you know it isn't), we think whatever they are asking sounds all right … then later we realise just what we have committed to.

On the other hand, if you rush in with an automatic no, you may regret it. Check your gut reaction to the request and also try to pinpoint the reason for your negative reaction.

You might have got into the habit of saying no in certain situations. You could be so used to stalling the kids' constant attempts to push the boundaries you have established that you don't stop to think that maybe time has moved on and you could make some concessions.

You might always say no without thinking when your shopping companion suggests you try a different colour, but suppose for once you said okay? Your habitual 'no' might be vindicated, but you just might discover that the particular shade of green matches your eyes or that you can actually wear a belt…ah, don't you look nice?

Your knee-jerk negative response might spring from fear if, for example, you are being asked to take on a demanding task at work or to make a presentation, to give a speech at a reception maybe or to attend a social occasion which sounds daunting.

It is possible that, on reflection, you might like to have a crack at the new project and feel pleased to have been asked. You might gear up to give the presentation – after all, it will help your career prospects and you'll have to get used to it some time. The same goes for the speech. As for the social occasion – you are grown up now, what's to daunt? You know how to put on the right clothes, slap on your face and get out there.

In theory, it is easier to say no and then say you have changed your mind than it is to agree to something and then pull out. In practice, there is not much in it. Once you have said no, you have taken up your position, you are perceived in a certain way, and the other person moves on and makes different arrangements. It can be quite difficult to retract a no, so check you really want to deliver one.

Get into the habit of the automatic pause. Wait just a moment or two before you speak. This strategy will keep you out of all kinds of trouble. Don't you just wish you'd done this when … ? You know when!

Be receptive

As you pause, listen and give the appearance of listening. Raise your eyebrows a bit, nod and smile just a little. Even if you don't like what you are hearing, it matters enough to the other person to have made them ask, and in some circumstances someone might have plucked up a lot of courage to approach you with a request. So it doesn't hurt to be gracious. You might like to accompany your receptive expression with a murmur of oh, ooh or ah as your brain clicks into gear and starts to process what is being proposed.

Repeat the request

This gives you a little more time and confirms that you have heard correctly.

+ *'So you want me to come over and look after the kids right now.'*

+ *'Right, you'd like me to take on Jason's workload while he's on holiday.'*

+ *'So, the cinema and a pizza.'*

+ *'So you're asking me to sponsor you to run a marathon.'*

Control your body language

Even if your heartfelt reaction is that you would rather have some grisly form of medieval torture than do what is being asked, don't let this show on your face. Do *not* smile encouragingly, as this will give the wrong impression, but don't frown and shake your head as the person is speaking. Keep your expression serious and immobile and nod just once to show understanding, not agreement. Make sure your voice is neutral, not heavily or even lightly sarcastic.

Get the details

Sometimes we are so eager to be nice and obliging that we say yes to a request when we have hardly even taken in the details of what has been asked. In our desire to be seen as Ms Can-Do or Ms Everyone's-Friend we make it almost a point of honour not to be fazed by a request.

We believe any sign of hesitation will be taken as a negative response and will indicate we are not really an on-board team player. So we open our mouths before engaging our brains and find we have agreed to go on a hen night that turns out to be a weekend in a spa hotel in Dubrovnik, to child-mind on a day when we had other plans, to make cupcakes for the fund-raiser when we thought we were just helping out at a stall, to give a 'short' presentation which turns out to need hours and hours of preparation and we're already over-committed ...

You could ask:

+ 'How much time do you think would be involved?'

+ 'What exactly do you want me to do?'

+ 'What kind of support is available?'

That way, you know what will be involved, and you can then decide whether you want to get involved or not.

Apologise

A brief, sincere 'sorry' is absolutely the right thing in most circumstances. But don't grovel and don't embellish the word with qualifiers about just how sorry you are – ever so, really, awfully. Just don't say them.

When you lead with this word, the person knows a refusal is coming. Sometimes you don't even need to say anything further – simply a 'sorry' accompanied by a shake of the head does the business. When you are about to say more, don't let your apologetic word dominate. You are sincere, but probably not desperately sorry. This isn't a heartfelt expression of deep regret, it is just social shorthand that keeps encounters smooth and courteous.

Show understanding

You have already repeated the facts or checked that you have understood. Now, where appropriate, show that you understand the person's situation and why the request is being made. This statement might begin with a phrase such as:

+ *I see that … you need help to organise the event.*

+ *I understand that … you are stuck for someone to look after the kids.*

+ *I realise that ... you need this urgently.*

+ *I appreciate that ... you need to find someone to do Jason's work.*

+ *I know that ... you'd get there more quickly if I drove you.*

+ *I get that ... you would like me to join you all.*

+ *I agree that ... the cinema and a pizza are an option.*

The 'no' word

This is the point at which you make your refusal clear and plain. It is likely that the other person has heard the 'but' in your voice and has seen it in your body language. Even though they are prepared for a refusal, 'but' can sound quite dismissive and has the effect of making someone ignore anything that has gone on before. If you find it hard to say 'but', try a linking phrase such as 'the thing is' or 'here's the situation', 'I have to tell you' or 'however'.

These phrases are easy to say and lead the way for a gentle but firm refusal. The other possibility is to slip the word 'but' in between a full statement of empathy and your refusal.

Then you say no. There are different ways of indicating refusal, but if you have any doubt at all about your ability to get your point across, make sure the actual word 'no' is spoken. Many people will be all too ready not to hear it.

✦ *'I understand that you need someone to help with the event and am pleased that you thought of me. The thing is, Davy, I have to say no.'*

✦ *'I can see that you're stuck for a sitter, and I'm sorry about that, but I'm afraid it has to be a no.'*

✦ *'I appreciate your thinking of me and it does sound like an interesting evening. However, I'm going to have to say no.'*

✦ *A 'no' in the middle of your sentence sounds gentle. Just make sure that you don't bury it among the other words.*

✦ *'I realise that you're strapped for cash at the moment and that must be very hard for you, but no, I'm not going to lend you the money.'*

Other phrases for 'no' are:

✦ *I'm going to pass on this occasion.*

✦ *That's not going to work for me.*

✦ *Sorry, not this time.*

✦ *I'm choosing not to.*

✦ *Thanks, but no thanks.*

✦ *Thanks, but not this time.*

✦ *I really don't want to do that.*

✦ *I don't think so.* (Watch your tone with this.)

Be upfront about your feelings

Tune into your emotional reaction to the request and your planned refusal. In some circumstances you might feel embarrassed about saying no. You might feel anxious that the relationship will be harmed. You might fear that someone will see hurt where none was intended.

Own your feelings. It is an honest, assertive thing to do, and it also pre-empts an attack from the other person as you are the first to say what may immediately occur to him or her.

PICTURE THIS

A friend or family member lent you his or her car for a week when you were in desperate need of transport. Now that person wants to borrow your car as his or hers is off the road. You consider this person not to be a safe driver.

TRY THIS

'You know, Matt, I feel embarrassed saying this because you were great and lent me a car that time, but I'm afraid it's a no.'

Excuses, reasons and lies

An excuse is what you come up with to get out of doing something, whereas a reason is an explanation. You know what a lie is, and it could be either of these.

A reason is assertive, an excuse is not. An excuse lacks conviction and confidence and often sounds lame. A reason is upfront and adds strength to your refusal.

You don't have to offer any information, you can say no and leave it at that.

It is up to you to choose how much explanation you give for your refusal. You are not obliged to explain yourself but in many cases you may choose to give a reason, simply to oil the wheels of the encounter.

You can be the judge of how much or how little you say – your choice will be influenced by the context, the circumstances and the relationship.

When it is appropriate to give a reason for a refusal, keep it brief. If you say too much, you run the risk of talking your way into saying yes, and you may give the other person a number of opportunities to break in and try to persuade you.

For example, if you are asked to take something on and you are not able to fit it in, don't start to describe all the things that you have to do. With a friendly or social request, this can make you sound a bit full of yourself, oh, look at busy me, and you don't want that. At work, it can make you seem all that as well as stressed and out of control – not a good look.

For example, if you say, 'Well, I would chair the committee, but it's frantic at the moment with all Doug's stuff to finish, then I've got those figures to get out, not to mention the monthly returns', you will sound stressed and out of control – and you will also give an opportunity for someone to say, 'Oh, don't worry about Doug's stuff, they cancelled ten minutes ago, so that frees up time for you to take on this new role.'

If your reason for not taking it on was genuine, you might be pleased with this development. If it was an excuse, you are rumbled.

That is the trouble with excuses: they are full of holes. You say you cannot make a dinner party because you have something else on that evening – your hosts reschedule. You say you cannot go to the book club meeting because you have to look after children or grandchildren – the leader offers the services of her daughter to do it for you.

Much safer and easier to give a catch-all reply which is not detailed and which makes the refusal clear.

PICTURE THIS

You are asked to take on a task or a role you don't want to do because you are already up to your eyes.

TRY THIS

'Although it does sound interesting/my kind of thing, I'm sorry to have to say no. My schedule's completely full at the moment.'

PICTURE THIS

You receive an invitation on a date you cannot make and you don't want to say what it is you are doing.

TRY THIS

'Thanks, but I'll have to pass as I've already made plans.'

PICTURE THIS

You are asked to go on holiday with another person, group or family and you don't want to go.

TRY THIS

'That's a lovely suggestion! The thing is, I/we really want to keep my/our options open about the summer/half-term/weekend, so it has to be a regretful no.'

When it is a 'maybe'

Ask for time

Be upfront about needing to think it over. There is no need to treat every request that comes your way as if it were a matter of life and death, but thinking about it shows that you are taking the request seriously.

It's a good idea to repeat the request. This shows that you have taken it on board and are willing to think about it. Be ready with a reply that shows you have understood what has been asked and which indicates how you will consider it.

But only do this when you genuinely mean it. If you are just stalling because you cannot say no straight away, then you are storing up problems for yourself.

Choose from these phrases

- ✦ *I need time to think about this.*

- ✦ *This is important – I need time to give it a lot of thought.*

- ✦ *That sounds like fun! I'll get back to you in ten minutes/ a week …*

- ✦ *I need ten minutes to sort out a few things before I give you an answer.*

- ✦ *If you need an answer right now, it's a no, but if you ask in a week or so, it might be different.*

- ✦ *I need to check my diary.*

- ✦ *I need to check out a few things at home before I give you a definite reply.*

Give a definite indication of when and how you will reply. Make it clear if you need a minute, a week or a month to think it over. Say if you will phone, text, email, drop by or write a note.

When you mean 'no', but give the impression of 'maybe'

Asking questions of any kind can give the impression that you are interested. If you really mean 'no', but are stalling for time while you psych yourself up to say it, you are being unfair to the other person.

Responses such as 'I'm not sure', 'It depends' or 'Have you asked anyone else?' open the door a little and encourage the requester to keep digging. If you definitely mean 'no', don't respond in this way.

A straightforward 'no'

There are some occasions when you need to give an outright 'no', without any discussion or expression of empathy.

These occasions may include refusing to give permission or to bend the rules for someone at home or at work, or saying no to an invitation or suggestion where no further explanation or acknowledgement is necessary.

Or there may be situations in which you just don't want to talk about your decision. You might not need to give this kind of direct response very often, but when you do, you can make your point firmly in a way that indicates that you are not open to argument or negotiation.

PICTURE THIS

Your daughter wants to stay overnight at her friend's house. You realise that the parents won't be there. You have already said she can go to sleepovers only if an adult is present. You have made it clear that this is non-negotiable.

TRY THIS

You say, 'No, Ellie, you can't go' or 'Ellie, the answer is no' or 'Ellie, you know the rule on this. You can't go.'

PICTURE THIS

Someone wants you to sign a petition for a cause to which you are opposed. You don't want to discuss the issue, you just want to refuse.

TRY THIS

You say, 'No, I'm not willing/going to sign this.'

PICTURE THIS

You are asked to contribute to a leaving present for someone you hardly know. You are short of money at the moment and don't want to do this.

TRY THIS

You say, 'You know, I've never actually spoken to Joe. I'll pass on the contribution and make a point of finding him to wish him all the best.'

When someone persists

The temptation is to give in under the pressure – but this would set a bad precedent if people realise that all they have to do is to ask you again. You need to repeat your refusal, if necessary, a little more firmly.

PICTURE THIS

Your friend wants you to join a Zumba class. This really is not your thing, but she is persistent because she doesn't want to go alone.

TRY THIS

'I'm sorry that you might have to go by yourself, but it really isn't something that I want to do.'

'Maybe you're right and I would enjoy it once I got there, but you know, it really isn't something that I want to do.'

When it doesn't work

You should only have to use the repetition once or twice. If the person keeps persisting – remember the vinyl record? The way to get the needle unstuck was to give it a gentle nudge, which moved it on. If they persist and you persist, you enter a stalemate. You might want to think about the extent and depth of the need behind the request. Why are they being so persistent?

You could ask, 'You know, Tara, it seems very important to you that we both do this?'

If she dismisses this comment and says it is no big deal, you can both drop it. You have made your point.

If she gives an indication that it does matter very much, you make your choice. You can repeat your core phrase, which should definitely be an end to the matter, or you could try to understand her thoughts and feelings and begin to negotiate or compromise.

Hey, what's to lose? A great workout to some sassy music, a good laugh, followed by a recuperative glass of red or a Mojito – see you there!

How to say no at work and still impress

There are generally two kinds of 'no' in work situations. There is 'No, not now' and 'No, never.' The former situations occur when someone wants you to do something urgently or wants you to do something that you cannot take on at that moment, but might at another point. The 'over my dead body' situations are the ones where you definitely want to refuse a suggestion or a request.

In both cases, an attitude of cooperation and negotiation will help you say no, but, at the same time, you will still be regarded as a team player and a supportive person. In fact, you will enhance your status and your reputation if you handle requests pleasantly and professionally.

When you are interrupted

When someone bursts in with a request for you to stop what you are doing and photocopy this document, make this phone call or send this email, assuming you are not contractually obliged to jump to every request, you need to give a clear message: 'No, not now.'

Remind yourself that it is absolutely fine to say this. In fact, it is the professional way to handle the situation.

Move quickly into what you can do and when you can do it.

If you need to give a reason, don't go into detail.

Don't use an expression like 'busy' – people hate it – and don't use an expression like 'up to my eyes', which only sounds ditzy and flustered.

PICTURE THIS

You are in a busy college office trying to finish a mail shot which has to go that day. Someone wants you to make 150 photocopies of a map he needs for a lesson.

TRY THIS

'I appreciate your situation, Miles. It's a no for right now, but what I can do is get them done by nine o'clock tomorrow.'

PICTURE THIS

You are asked to take on a task or a role you don't want to do because you are already up to your eyes.

TRY THIS

'I'll have to say no, I'm afraid – my time is fully committed at the moment.'

When you have to disappoint someone

It can be hard to say no to someone who has asked for a pay rise, promotion or a change in conditions. Acknowledge the person's contribution and empathise with their disappointment. Give a clear reason for your decision. Don't get sidelined into having a chat about it.

PICTURE THIS

You are turning down your assistant's request to be given the responsibility for organising a major event.

TRY THIS

'Max, I have to tell you that I've decided to say no to your request. I don't think you're ready for such a big project. I'm sorry to disappoint you on this occasion.'

The power of 'no'

Practise saying the word 'no'. You might like to do this in front of a mirror or with a trustworthy friend who will give you feedback. Relax your head and your facial muscles.

Remember you can say yes

Learning how to say no can be invigorating and liberating, especially if your reluctance to deal with requests or demands has had damaging consequences. Use your new ability when you need to. Don't use it to exercise your power or as a vehicle for self-protection.

If there are situations in which your automatic reflex is to say no, think about your reasons. You could have a knee-jerk reaction to particular people or particular types of request.

If you see your boss as someone who always makes unreasonable demands, know that your child constantly pushes at the boundaries in order to wear you down or that a friend is always trying to rope you in to some volunteering project, you might be ready to say no without listening properly to what they are saying or without considering the consequences of saying yes.

You can say no to your boss, but what would happen if you said yes, on certain conditions? You can say to your teenager that no, he can't go out until he's tidied his bedroom, or no, she can't go to a concert on a school night – but you could also decide to say yes. You could think, 'What's the worst that can happen?' and count up how many Brownie points you will get for being fab.

·

CHAPTER SEVEN

Dealing with Criticism

GIVING CRITICISM, offering constructive criticism, giving negative feedback – however we phrase it, we are talking about pointing out to someone what they are doing wrong, how they are failing in some way, how they are not meeting our expectations or how they are displeasing us.

We let them know their shortcomings and just how they are getting things wrong. We express our disapproval all the time, in hundreds of ways. We sigh heavily, we look exasperated, we snap at people, we have tiffs, rows, arguments and disagreements.

Or we don't. Sometimes we don't give any outward sign that we are upset by someone's behaviour. We bottle up our feelings and try not to let our emotions show. It may be that we don't quite know how to put into words what is bothering us. It may be that we don't trust ourselves to speak without losing control completely, bursting into tears or physically hitting out. We think we will sound stupid.

Or we tell ourselves that it doesn't really matter, it's not worth saying anything. When we do this, sisters, we are telling the worst kind of lie – a lie to ourselves.

'Criticism' is a heavy word. It is not one we want associated with us. When we see other people in these terms, it is usually negative: 'Harry's so nit-picking,' we think, dreading what he will think of our idea, or 'I won't ask Sadie what she thinks of the new kitchen because she's always so critical.' We wouldn't like anyone thinking of us as someone who is ready to find fault. We don't want to be accused of being a nag.

The word 'criticism' carries connotations of being told off, of being shouted at and of having an admonitory finger waved in our face. The very word can transport us back to younger versions of ourselves when we felt at the receiving end of a stream of critical comments about our behaviour and our appearance – skirts too short or too long, heels too high or too clumpy, don't speak to me like that, watch your manners, young lady…

It takes us back to the days of being put in detention at school, of being grounded or having our pocket money stopped.

We can move on from the hard-edged notion of 'criticism'. We are too grown-up for tellings-off, giving them or receiving them. Think instead of dialogue and communication which is rich in every way, in which you can confidently express your thoughts and feelings and share your perceptions, positive and negative, in an appropriate way which enhances and develops the quality of your relationships and experiences.

What it means

What do we do when we 'give criticism'? We explain to somebody that what they are doing, a way they are behaving, is upsetting, hurting or damaging us in some way – or perhaps just inconveniencing us, or causing us annoyance or irritation. We let somebody know that what they are doing or have done isn't meeting our expectations.

These expectations might be a standard of performance in the workplace, or a standard of behaviour that is spoken or unspoken, which may be applied to a diverse range

of situations.If you stick to these parameters, the idea of saying something negative becomes less overwhelming. You are not being unpleasant, nasty or horrible. You are not having a pop at someone. You do not intend to inflict hurt, pain or embarrassment.

Good reasons for keeping quiet

You don't have to communicate every thought and every emotion that troubles you. There are occasions when swallowing a big glass of shut-up juice is the best thing to do. What you need to do is check your reasons for keeping quiet. You might consider buttoning it up when:

The behaviour in question is mildly annoying and your annoyance quickly subsides.

Try a scale of 1–10 for the magnitude of the behaviour. How much does it matter? If it is below 5, you might want to let it go for now. How lasting is its effect? Again, if the number is less than 5, you could consider putting it on the back burner for now and reconsider if it happens again.

You won't gain anything from expressing your feelings.

There are occasions when nothing will be gained: not only is it impossible to change or rectify a situation, but you won't even feel any better for speaking out.

You have had recent or frequent 'critical' encounters with this person.

You could decide to not reply immediately, but to have a conversation about the situation at a later time.

Even though you may be perfectly justified in what you feel like saying, you might want to examine the nature of your encounters with the individual and, if they have been unremittingly critical, pause and think about how to balance your communication.

In every case, remember: just because you can doesn't mean you have to.

Bad reasons for keeping quiet

It is hardly worth bringing up

Even if your annoyance is above the middle of the 1–10 scale, you might think the actual behaviour, the thing that is getting to you, is too trivial to bring up. Not so.

If it is bothering you this much, it doesn't matter how slight it may seem. In your domestic arena, someone's habit of leaving dirty dishes all over the kitchen or complaining when you do the same can seem like a fuss about nothing, but when we share living spaces, habits and routines play an important part in our well-being.

If a friend or family member is always late for appointments, cancels arrangements at the last minute or keeps looking at their watch when you are talking to them, you may feel they are showing a lack of concern or respect for you and this will have an effect on your relationship.

It is not the behaviour itself that is the point. What matters is how you react to it and the way it affects you.

Being scared of what will happen

If you take this approach, you relinquish control to other people. You allow your perception of their feelings to dominate and shape your relationship, and you make yourself miserable by maintaining an unsatisfactory situation because of an unfounded fear of the consequences of open communication.

Be prepared, not scared. You can present your feelings in a way which will not cause offence and which will clear up misunderstandings. Something will change, however. That's the point. All change can be uncomfortable, even changes that are welcome, so be ready to adjust to slightly different relationships. Different but better. Well-placed, sensitively delivered requests about changing behaviour will lead to more understanding and respect. That's good, isn't it?

The negative effects of bottling it up

If you keep a lid on your feelings and allow little niggles and resentments to build up until they become huge, the chances are that one day you will explode with anger or frustration. The damaging effects of this kind of explosion far outweigh the initial discomfort of giving some negative feedback.

The strain of suppressing your feelings can cause stress and tension and affect your mental well-being. You might feel you are keeping things peaceful but you are storing up trouble for yourself and your personal and working relationships.

When expressing criticism is the best option

Once you have decided that the right thing to do is to express your problem or grievance, don't just blurt it out. Think through what you want to say and how you are going to say it. Apply the same process of preparation no matter who the person is or what the circumstance and give each situation the same degree of thought and respect.

Identify the core issue

When something is getting to you, try to identify the root cause of your feelings. Sometimes your irritation with an easily identifiable surface behaviour is a sign of deeper dissatisfaction or concern. For example, you feel critical of the way your son is dressing but your real concern is he is dressing like his new group of friends who you don't like.

Identify your motives

There are two primary motives for expressing criticism:

1. You would like the other person to change their behaviour in some way. You would like them to stop doing something, to start doing something or to start doing something in a different way.

2. You want to express your dissatisfaction, anger, irritation or annoyance in a situation where asking for change is inappropriate. In these circumstances, you want to say something that is on your mind, even though nothing can be done to alter events.

There are other motives that need not detain us here. You might just need to have a hack at someone, you might want to get back at someone or make him or her feel uncomfortable.

You might have a go at an individual because they are weaker than you, they won't answer back or just because you can.

None of these describes assertive grown-up behaviour, so none will apply to you, isn't that so?

Make your point

Decide exactly what you are going to ask for. Whatever it is, present your case in a way which leaves room for discussion and allows the other person appropriate space and flexibility. Think of this as a three-part process: you describe the situation, you say how you feel and how it is affecting you, and you put forward the change that you would like.

Describe the behaviour

Be specific about the behaviour you are criticising. It is the behaviour, not the person; the deed, not the doer; the sin, not the sinner.

Don't go in for a general character assassination but focus on what is concrete and observable. So it's not 'He's so thoughtless', but 'He makes arrangements for us both without checking if they are all right by me'. It's not 'She's so bitchy', but 'She makes unkind and hurtful remarks.' In your head, replace 'He's an attention-grabbing, self-centred, self-promoter' with ' He took all the credit for our joint project.'

Keep your description short and unemotional. This means avoiding generalisations such as 'always' and 'never'. These blanket terms express your frustration or annoyance, but they are rarely accurate and they weaken the impact of your case.

Don't use judgmental language or highly coloured descriptions. Saying 'You go around as if you own the place' or 'When you flounced out of the room' will put the other person on the defensive and may lead to the conversation being sidetracked into the unproductive 'No, I don't/didn't,' 'Yes, you do/did' area.

Don't be a mind-reader. Avoid phrases such as 'You seem to think ...' or 'You tried to make me feel stupid.' Other phrases to avoid are expressions such as 'The trouble with you is ...'

Identify your feelings about the behaviour

Take some time to identify as precisely as you can how you are being affected. Do you feel annoyed or angry? Upset, hurt, humiliated? Frustrated, worried, anxious? Fed up, furious, bored? Put-upon, exploited, taken for granted? 'I'm not angry, I'm just hurt,' sang the Everly Brothers in their sweet, soaring, melodic voices. But they hoped that the girl who left them would tear her brand new dress, would wear shoes that made her feet ache, would have a car that wouldn't start ... that wasn't just hurt, they were pretty angry. The shoes in particular. We wouldn't wish bunions and corns on our worst enemy – well, maybe just a teensy one on the little toe …

You might choose not to communicate the real depth of your response. In a work situation, for example, or with someone not very close to you, you could use a bland word or expression such as 'concerned' or 'surprised', 'put out' or 'disturbed'.

Think about the other person's point of view

You may have lived with this issue for some time. It is possible that the person you are talking to is not aware there is a problem or does not realise how much it is affecting you. They may not respond in the way that you imagine, so be prepared for the unexpected.

Describe how the behaviour affects you

This is a crucial step in creating understanding because this is where you make clear why it matters. If you have got nothing to say here, if you cannot express just why you are feeling this way, then stop and think again about your reasons for raising the matter.

If you say straight away how you are affected, you forestall the other person having to ask, which he or she could do in a challenging way, so it is a good idea to make your point first. So, 'I feel annoyed and frustrated when you cancel at the last minute because then it's too late for me to make other plans' is clearer than 'It's so annoying when you cancel at the last minute'.

Asking for a change (if appropriate)

When you would like specific change in someone's behaviour, this is where you say what you want. In some situations it will be something straightforward, especially if rules and procedures, at home or at work, are involved.

Whatever the change is, make it clear and concrete and put it in positive terms. Don't say what you want them to stop doing – say what you would like them to do instead. Rather than 'Don't be late in future,' say, 'You need to be in by such-and-such a time.' Instead of 'I would like you to stop giving me tasks at the last minute' say, 'I'd like to have some notice of jobs so that I can organise my time.'

PICTURE THIS

When you go to your partner's work do, he or she spends a lot of time talking shop with other people, while you are left alone, which you don't like at all.

TRY THIS

'You know, I'm not looking forward to next week's do at the club. I understand that it's a good opportunity for you to catch up with people, but when you leave me by myself, I feel awkward and self-conscious. I'd like it if you would limit conversations that exclude me.'

When you don't want to ask for a change

Sometimes you may need to ask someone to stop a certain behaviour and leave it at that. If you are at the receiving end of put-downs or spiteful remarks, you might just say, 'I don't appreciate these comments, and I would like you to stop making them.'

What you might want to add is that you want the person to start treating you with respect and recognise you for the goddess that you are. Think it, but don't say it. You are leading the way. They will learn.

It might be the case that you are still fuming about something that has happened and cannot be changed. The best thing would really be to accept the situation and move on. If you think you cannot do that until you have expressed your feelings to the appropriate person, then say something like 'I realise that nothing can be done about the new arrangements but I need to tell you that I feel the consultation was rushed and inadequate. That's all I want to say.'

Ask for feedback

Get the other person's reaction. Ask if they understand your point. Use phrases such as 'What do you think?' or 'How does that sound to you?'

Listen to what they have to say. Be prepared to change your point of view if they offer a different perspective on the matter. Many of us hit back when we feel we are under attack. We'll say things like 'What about you? You can talk!', 'It's not just me' or 'It isn't fair.'

If you think they may have a point about your behaviour, agree, but don't get drawn into discussing it. You could say, 'Yes, I know I can be thoughtless as well, but right now I want to talk about ...'

If you think they have a point about someone else, just acknowledge what they have said in a general way: 'It may be the case that Gerry always does the same, but right now we're talking about ...'

PICTURE THIS

You have said your bit about the work do. Your partner says, 'You shouldn't feel awkward! And it's a good opportunity for me to make some contacts.'

TRY THIS

'Maybe I shouldn't feel awkward, but I do. I want to be included in conversations. I'll enjoy the evening much more if I join in with you.'

Moving on

At the end of the conversation, you both need to know where you stand. Where appropriate, specify any consequences that will arise if things don't change. In work situations there may be precise outcomes such as taking further action or referring the matter to another person. This may also apply to your personal life.

PICTURE THIS

You host a big family occasion and although your siblings offer to help, they end up having a good time while you do all the donkey work. You have spoken about this before but nothing changes. You are really fed up with the situation.

TRY THIS

'I love having everyone here, but I really am not prepared to carry on doing all the work by myself. We need to find a way of spreading it out. If we can't agree and stick to a different arrangement, then we'll have to find somewhere else for Laura's engagement party.'

How to begin and end a critical conversation

Useful phrases to flag up your intention:

+ *There's something I need to tell you.*

+ *There's something that's bothering me.*

+ *There's something we need to discuss.*

+ *I'd like to talk to you about something.*

Useful phrases to end your discussion:

+ *I'm glad we've sorted that out.*

+ *It's good to have cleared the air.*

+ *Thanks for that. I feel much better now that we've talked about it.*

Useful phrases for introducing a criticism of someone's behaviour:

✦ *You might not be aware of it, but ...*

✦ *I'm sure you don't mean it to be seen this way, but ...*

Phrases to avoid:

✦ *And another thing ...*

✦ *And while we're on the subject ...*

✦ *I'm fed up with you doing ...*

✦ *I've just about had enough of your ...*

Time and place

You need to feel in control of yourself and your emotions when you initiate this kind of difficult conversation. If you are feeling down or tired, hungry or drunk, or if you are in any physical or mental state that affects your mood and energy level, don't embark on it.

Think about the other person's mood as well. Even though you will handle the discussion beautifully and show respect and empathy for the other person, it could still be hard for them to take, and they may want to think more about what you have said, so be careful with your timing.

You might spend all day psyching yourself up to say something, but it may not be a good idea to let it all out as soon as your target walks through the door. Don't bring up negative stuff just before going out for the evening or when someone is upset or agitated about another matter.

At the other end of the scale, you might choose not to rain on their parade at a time when they are in a cheerful, upbeat mood.

You can choose the circumstances in which you discuss such matters, too. All conversations are affected by the context in which they take place. Some critical conversations need the gravitas of a formal situation; others can be held at the kitchen table, over a meal or a drink (steady there if it's an alcoholic drink), on a walk, in a quiet place at work, in your work space, in their work space, while you are cooking, driving …

Talking while driving can work well when you want to bring up an issue with a youngster. The movement of the car is soothing, the scenery is distracting and looking straight ahead may be less embarrassing or awkward for them than a face-to-face talk.

How to handle being criticised

Let's face it, it never feels good. Whether it comes out of the blue, taking you by surprise, or is something you are prepared for, you are likely to react as if you are under attack – which, in a way, you are. Your heart thumps, you feel a bit shaky, and you want to hit back at the person who is speaking or run away and hide. But you can deal with criticism or negative comments in a mature way.

Stay calm

The key to handling these situations with grace and confidence is to remain calm. So if you are knocked for six, cannot think straight and feel as if you are going to burst into tears, don't respond. Say something like 'I need to think about this. Can we talk about it later?' and remove yourself from the situation.

Accept what is being said

Your instinct when hearing something unpleasant or difficult might be to stick your fingers in your ears and chant 'La, la, la, can't hear you.'

Be brave. A helpful strategy is to view the message as information that someone is giving you, information that, if processed properly, will help you personally and will help your relationship.

You could even think of what is being said as an offering: someone is sufficiently connected to you and involved with you to want to take the difficult step of telling you something that you may not wish to hear or something you were unaware of.

Criticism is truly constructive when it leads to a better situation. You might not have been aware that your partner hates it when you have long phone conversations with your pals or your sister in the evening.

Your partner might not be aware how irritating you find his or her constant playing games on their iPhone (or as they would have it, doing important research). When a negative aspect of your behaviour is brought to your attention, no matter how strange it may seem to you, take a moment to see the situation from the other person's viewpoint and get inside their skin.

Listen and check understanding

Hear the words and repeat them. Speak calmly and ignore the tone in which they were said. This will help keep your communication on an even keel. Check that you have received the intended message:

+ *'OK, I understand you feel upset because I didn't invite you to the wine tasting evening.'*

+ *'You're angry because I forgot to pick up the dry cleaning.'*

+ *'So you're saying that I'm not a team player.'*

You might need to clarify:

+ *'Are you saying that I always leave you out of the arrangements or are you talking about last weekend?'*

Check for motives

Assess what is behind this information. If it is honest feedback, although it might not quite tie up with the way that you yourself see the situation, be prepared to deal with it seriously. If you can tell that someone is just having a pop at you, don't waste your energy responding. Just say something like 'Oh, I don't think so,' 'That's not the way I see it' or 'Not where I'm standing from' and forget it.

When you are not sure what is behind a comment

Sometimes you feel a critical view is being implied, although nothing specific is said. You have two choices: you can choose to believe or to respond as if you believe no criticism is intended, or you can ask for more information.

The kind of ambiguous comment you might experience could be offerings such as:

+ *'Is that what you're wearing?'*

+ *'Did you go to a different hairdresser?'*

+ *'Is that new?'*

+ *'Did you make this yourself?'*

If you want to reply as if you haven't suspected a word of criticism, give a brief 'Yes' or 'No' and change the subject immediately, leaving no room for any further discussion.

If you want to flush out what the speaker means, ask a question. Be careful to keep your voice neutral and not to sound aggressive or defensive.

Useful answers

Answers that ask for more information:

✦ *'Yes, this is what I've decided to wear. Why do you ask?'*

✦ *'No, the same hairdresser as usual/Yes, the person who usually does it has left. Does my hair look different?'*

✦ *'You're right, it is new/No, not particularly new. Why do you ask?'*

✦ *'Yes, it's all my own work/No, I didn't make it myself. Does it matter?'*

This kind of response might result in a critical comment, so be prepared for this and decide how you will deal with it.

Alternatively, you might get a reply like 'Oh, I just wondered', which is actually pretty manipulative, designed to make you feel as if there is something wrong without it being actually spelt out. In these circumstances, you could regain control of the situation by saying very pleasantly something non-committal such as 'Fine' or 'Okay'. If you want to nail the point that is being criticised (but why bring it on yourself, unless it is important that you know), you could say, 'You sound as if you don't like it' and see what information you get. But hey, if it is just someone trying to unsettle you, why give him or her the satisfaction?

Answers that deflect criticism
If your reply firmly shows that you view the matter at issue in a positive light, you make it difficult for someone to be critical.

✦ *'Yes, this is the dress I've decided to wear. I feel good in it.'*

✦ *'Same/Different hairdresser. I really like the way he's done the highlights.'*

✦ *'Yes, I bought it recently and I'm loving it'/'No, I've had it some time. I wouldn't be without it.'*

✦ *'Yes, I made it myself/No, I didn't make it myself, and I'm so pleased with the way it turned out.'*

Accept responsibility

If the criticism is absolutely valid, hold your hands up and admit it:

✦ *'You're right, that was a careless mistake.'*

✦ *'Yes, I can see that I should have checked the figures before submitting the report.'*

✦ *'I could have thought twice before telling that joke about bankers.'*

Keep your acceptance brief and to the point. Don't start to beat yourself up: 'Oh, I'm so hopeless at this kind of thing/ That's me all over, isn't it/I'm a rotten friend, aren't I.'

If you want to do something about the aspect that is under scrutiny, you may like to add a reassurance that shows you will behave differently in future: 'I will be more careful/thorough/thoughtful next time.'

If you don't intend to change, either say nothing or acknowledge the 'fault': 'I know I tend to leave things until the last minute – I like the rush'/'I can be a bit careless with detail – to tell you the truth, I get bored going over the nuts and bolts of something.'

Add value

You could make the exchange more productive by asking for help or ideas about ways you could make things better: 'You're right, I haven't been very supportive of Fran. Can you think of something I could do to help?'

Get it in balance

If you are being criticised for something that isn't typical of you, say so: 'I'm sorry you thought the restaurant was an expensive choice for some of the group. I'm usually thoughtful of people's different circumstances.'

Apologise

A brief apology is often appropriate. Make sure that you apologise for the relevant factor, which is the harm, discomfort or inconvenience you have caused someone. Say:

'I'm sorry you had to wait because I was late', not: 'Sorry I'm such a rubbish timekeeper.'

When you need to make up for something

If your action or inaction has made things difficult for someone, you could ask if there is anything you can do: 'I'm sorry to have caused a delay. Can I do anything now to speed things up?'

Genuine but inaccurate criticism

If you completely disagree with something that is thrown at you, say so. But don't say it snappily. Take a pause, repeat the remark and say something like 'You know, I don't agree with that at all. I wonder what I've done to give you the impression that I'm lazy/two-faced/unfair?'

Listen to the answer. You might learn something about how your behaviour affects others. If you can see where the other person is coming from, say so: 'I can see how I might have appeared like that. But I don't agree that I am ...'

Self-protection

We respond most forcefully to criticism that refers to those aspects of our person that matter most to us. If being tidy or reliable, inconsiderate or a good cook doesn't matter much to you, you are likely to handle criticism of your behaviour in these areas calmly. However, if it matters to you to be a reliable friend or a considerate colleague, you will feel uncomfortable when someone finds your behaviour in these respects wanting.

Being aware of the values and behaviours that are central to your person will help you control your response to criticism. Your automatic instinct in these cases may be a defensive, angry response. Recognise when this response starts to kick in and remind yourself to stay calm and listen to what is said.

PICTURE THIS

You try hard to get your kids to eat healthily. A friend notices them eating crisps and says, 'Are you happy with them eating that rubbish?'

TRY THIS

Take a breath and steady yourself. Tell yourself not to let the words get to you. Say something like 'I know they're eating crisps at the moment, but I see to it that they don't usually eat rubbish.'

CHAPTER EIGHT

Tricky Situations in Your Personal and Social Life

Answering difficult questions

No, not the ones about the meaning of life, the universe and the political problems of the Middle East – they are easy by comparison with the casual or not-so-casual enquiry that makes you wish that the ground would just open and swallow you up.

These kinds of question often occur in a social setting and involve people you are not particularly close to. Such questions are usually not in the least malicious, but they require you to reveal things that you would rather not talk about or they focus on the areas of your life that may be insecure and vulnerable at that moment.

Don't over-reveal

It is helpful to remind yourself you do not need to be completely honest. We know assertiveness is all about openness and honesty but that does not mean complete and unabridged disclosure of everything that is going on.

You know what it is like when your casual 'How are you?' leads to half an hour in the supermarket aisle being taken through every moment of someone's bad day. And you were just being friendly.

You are not obliged to tell everyone your son failed his A levels or your partner has gone off with your best friend. You don't have to reveal you have had a row with your mother-in-law or your daughter-in-law, your boss or your neighbour, your stepchildren hate you or you have gained two stone since giving up smoking.

Prepare an answer

Sometimes we are taken completely by surprise but often we know we are likely to bump into certain people who will automatically ask particular questions or bring up particular subjects.

The kind of information being requested may well be, or be about to become, common knowledge and, however you answer, the facts will emerge.

The way you present your answer shows the 'official' line you want others to take. Whatever your private interpretation of and feelings about the subject, you can choose how you present it publicly. Building into your reply a hint that gives the enquirer an idea about where you stand on the issue not only protects you but also is courteous towards the other person, stopping him or her from putting their foot in it.

The following suggestions are for those occasions when you want to manage the encounter in a socially acceptable way without revealing much, if anything. An assertive response in these circumstances protects you from feeling pushed or persuaded into saying things you don't want to say.

Choose a suggestion that could work for you or adapt these ideas to formulate your own answer, and practise delivering it.

PICTURE THIS

You are happily single. People ask why you are not married.

TRY THIS

There are lots of snappy comebacks you could make to this kind of question, but you run the risk of sounding defensive or aggressive. We suggest keeping your reply pleasant and bland:

'I'm happy as I am. Thank you for caring/for your concern.' (said with a big smile)

'Absolutely no comment.' (said with a big smile)

'Classified information!' (said with a big smile)

You could use the above suggestions to queries about, for example, when you are going to have children or when you and your significant other are going to tie the knot.

If these comments are frequent and rate high on the offensiveness scale, you may need to tell the speaker to back off: 'You know, Claris, I would like you to stop asking me that.' Another 'back off' tactic is to make an enquiry: 'Oh, does it bother you?' (Keep your tone light.)

PICTURE THIS

You have very recently lost your job, and are feeling vulnerable about the future. Someone asks: 'Are you still teaching at …/working at …/running the accounts department …?'

TRY THIS

'Recession/Cuts/Cutbacks casualty, I'm afraid. There's a lot of it about.'

'Oh, I've moved on, actually. Heading for pastures new.'

If you are unemployed, you might say:

'Actually, I'm in a transitional phase at the moment. Looking for something new.'

'I'm in the middle of exploring my options.'

PICTURE THIS

Everyone assumes you will go back to work after having children but you don't want to. You don't want to sound defensive or apologetic about your decision.

TRY THIS

'I'm probably as surprised as you are, but I'm choosing not to go back to work right now.'

PICTURE THIS

Everyone assumes that you won't go back to work after having children, but you have decided to do so. You don't want to sound defensive or apologetic about your decision.

TRY THIS

'I know this may surprise you, but I've decided to go back to work, and I'm really comfortable with that decision.'

PICTURE THIS

You have failed or not done well in an exam. Someone asks: 'How did the exam go?'

TRY THIS

'A little disappointing, but nothing that won't work out.'

'Oh, just as expected, no surprises.'

If the question is more direct, such as 'What grades did you get in the exams?', you could answer:

'Oh, I'm absolutely delighted, thank you for asking.'

Then you add a soupçon of information to move the conversation along:

'And I've decided to concentrate on … next year.'

PICTURE THIS
You didn't get the job you applied for. Someone asks: 'Did you get that job?'

TRY THIS
'My name wasn't on that particular position, but there's a lot in the pipeline.'

'It wasn't the right move for me as it turned out'

PICTURE THIS
Your significant other is now an ex-significant other. Someone asks: 'How's so-and-so?'

TRY THIS
'Actually, we've split up, and you know, I don't like talking about it.'

'He/She is fine, but we're no longer together.'

'I've no idea, and actually I don't care.'

These ideas can be applied to questions about your family and friends. Instead of 'I', refer to the person in question.

PICTURE THIS
Your friend's/daughter's relationship has ended very unhappily. Someone asks 'When's Katie getting engaged?'

TRY THIS
'Oh, that didn't work out in the end. At the moment she's busy doing...'

Family stuff

The complicated mix of blood ties, affection, duty, expectations and familiarity that enriches family relationships can also curdle and sour them. It is particularly important where family members are concerned not to let gripes and resentments fester and grow.

You know how it is – the wrong thing said at the wrong time, something neglected or mishandled, a careless word or gesture and there you are, locked in a feud or standoff which makes the families of Greek tragedy (murder of parents and children, human sacrifice, cannibalism, to name but a few) look like *The Waltons*.

The dynamics of family behaviour and relationships can be challenging, to say the least. Whether you are part of a traditional or blended family unit, balancing your needs and wishes with those of children, partners, parents and siblings requires commitment, courage and delicate negotiation.

At times, dealing assertively with crucial issues seems to demand such energy that we give in and let things drift on, hoping that they will just work out.

Now and again things do sort themselves out, but if the issues at stake really matter, it is more likely that you will become resentful and frustrated both with yourself and with your family. The danger is that these feelings will build up until you explode with rage.

Taking an assertive approach to family problems will make your relationships stronger. Your bonds with family members are complex and enduring, and it makes sense to manage your relationships in a way that minimises conflict and misunderstandings.

Dealing with expectations

When it comes to those we are closest to, many of us fall into well-established patterns of behaviour. You don't know quite how it has turned out this way, but you always do the majority of the household chores. You are the one who reminds your siblings of significant birthdays and anniversaries, or you are the one who always has to be reminded of them.

You always take the lead in family discussions, or you always let more forceful family members have a strong voice. You always give in to your kids' requests because you don't want them complaining to your ex about you. You say no to their requests without really listening to them because your defence mechanism kicks in automatically.

These patterns may work for you. They may be a source of annoyance. If you decide you want to change something, choose a specific issue and circumstance.

PICTURE THIS

You have always cooked the evening meal in your household. Now, though, you have had enough of doing it all the time. You would like others to take a turn.

TRY THIS

'Listen, everyone, there's something I want you to think about. I'm happy to cook our evening meal, but not every evening.

I'd like to do the weekend meals, that's Friday to Sunday. Let's sort out who will take which days during the week.'

PICTURE THIS

You are annoyed because your partner gave permission for one of the kids to do something you had vetoed. It is not the first time this has happened.

TRY THIS

Decide what you are annoyed about. Is it the fact that you have been thwarted or that you feel you have been made to look like the bad guy? Are you feeling that your partner has deliberately undermined you? Are you feeling that your child has been manipulative?

Decide what outcome you want. Is it to force a block on the agreement? Is it to make sure that it doesn't happen in future?

Once you know what you feel and what you want, make a calm approach. Begin with an 'I' statement:

'I'm bothered/upset/angry/puzzled about ...' Then state what you want: 'I'd like to understand why/I'd like us to find a way of ...'

Juggling obligations

We know, we know, you don't need to feel obliged and you know all about getting rid of the 'shoulds' and 'oughts'. So you don't have to visit your parents, invite family round for Sunday lunch, babysit for your brother or sister, son or daughter, go to your cousin's wedding, go to the children or grandchildren's school concerts, and you could assertively state your intention of not doing so.

On the other hand, you could accept the element of obligations and expectations that are part of the web of family ties and manage them with grace, firmness and diplomacy.

PICTURE THIS

You have an elderly parent or parents who live independently, but require some help, which you and your siblings agree to provide. Because of geographical and personal circumstances, you cannot visit as often as you would like to. This causes resentment and misunderstandings.

TRY THIS

Identify your feelings about the situation. Banish guilt immediately, unless there is something to feel guilty about. Work out what you want. Do you want to be reassured that the others know you do your best to shoulder your share? Do you want to be informed about what goes on in your absence? Do you want to be involved in making decisions even though you won't be around much to see their effects? Maybe you want to find a way of making a different kind of contribution.

Once you know what you feel and what you would like, speak to your siblings, together and face to face. Acknowledge your feelings:

'I know this may sound silly but' or 'I feel awkward about this, but I'd like to tell you what I feel.'

Ask what *they* feel about the situation.

Don't get sidetracked into old feuds or grievances. Use the table tennis bat to lob these references into a safe place to be revisited at a later point if necessary.

Gifts and tokens

The exchanging of presents should be a joyous expression of affection, but may become a minefield of power plays, guilt and manipulation. The subtle matching of price, taste, intention can reveal gaps in our perception of each other and create patterns of obligation that cause anxiety and resentment.

You can break this pattern with assertive communication.

PICTURE THIS
A family member gives you a Christmas or birthday present that you just don't like and don't want.

TRY THIS
Well, you know the form now. You have the right to tell your mother-in-law that the nice notepaper and address book she gave you is useless because, duh, doesn't she know you are totally electronic now, or to ask your brother if his gift box set of romcoms is meant to be a reminder that you are unhappily single. You could make it clear the offering is unsuitable:

'That's so thoughtful of you. Actually, if you give me the receipt, I'll exchange it next week/I know you won't mind if I re-gift it …'

Or you could exercise your right not to be honest and choose to acknowledge what the gift represents: 'That's so thoughtful/kind/generous. Thank you.'

You could put your assertive skills to positive use by pre-empting the situation: 'You remember you gave me such-and-such last year? Well, just to keep you up to date, since then I've got more into vampire movies/cashmere gloves/beige or taupe colours/flowery mugs.'

Or you could suggest you should all exchange wish lists. You could also suggest a price range. That would be much better getting it wrong, at either end of the scale.

Dealing with visitors

What should be a source of pleasure can become the subject of argument or conflict. You and your partner might have different ideas about the nature and frequency of visits from friends and family members.

For you, the ring of the phone or the bell might herald fresh hell, as Dorothy Parker of the acid tongue observed, while for others it heralds an opportunity for fun. You might have different ideas about the kind of behaviour that is appropriate when you have visitors. Or your visitors might behave in ways you don't like.

PICTURE THIS

You have just had a baby, and your family and friends want to visit. You understand they are all dying to see the baby, and to see you but you really don't feel like it at the moment and want to be left alone.

TRY THIS

To people who you don't want to visit at all at the present, say something like 'I'd love you to come and see the baby, but right now isn't the best time. I'll be gagging for a visit in such-and-such a time, so let's fix up something then.'

With those close to you who are going to insist on a peek no matter what you say, set some boundaries. Say you are tired and you and the baby will have to disappear after half an hour or so. Indicate where the kettle and cups are. If you don't want your photo taken, say so. Pictures of your wonderful newborn posted all over Facebook is one thing but you have the right to veto images of you in your lank-haired, greasy-skinned, red-eyed postpartum state. (Oh, childbirth leaves you looking even more glowing and lovely than usual? Well, good for you!)

PICTURE THIS

Some of your family could be described as a lively bunch. You like having them round, but you feel uncomfortable when your kids hear their fruity language. At the same time, you don't want to sound prudish and uptight.

TRY THIS

When the situation arises, say something like 'Hey, can we tone it down in front of the kids?'

When they look astounded and ask tone down what, say that you just want to keep your kids as innocent as a mock-tail for as long as you can.

PICTURE THIS

One of your circle is in the habit of popping round at a time that clearly suits them, but doesn't suit you.

TRY THIS

The gracious thing is to let them know. Say something like 'It's lovely to see you, but this isn't a great time for a catch-up.' Then offer an alternative.

Assertive approaches to tricky situations in your friendship group

Smart girls take their friendships seriously. They value and celebrate their inner and outer circle of friends and take steps to maintain and nourish these ties.

Assertive behaviour will help these special relationships grow and flourish. Behaving in an open and engaging way will encourage similar responses and minimise the negative impact of everyday irritations and annoyances.

Feeling hurt or angry

We sometimes hurt each other. We are thoughtless and careless and give insufficient attention to how we affect those closest to us. As the song says, and has been saying from the 1940s to the present day, so it must be true: 'You always hurt the one you love.'

When you realise a deed or word has hurt someone, apologise – and do it right away. Don't think they'll get over it or they will realise you didn't mean anything or were only joking. They might do, but they might not.

When you are the one who is hurt or angry or irritated, say so. Don't let it fester. Choose the level at which you engage. Sometimes just a little 'Ouch, that hurt!' will do. There may be some occasions when you want to talk at greater length about a situation. Only by talking will you reach an understanding and be in a position to move on from what has upset you.

Way back earlier than the 1940s, the great poet and prophet William Blake had it nailed: 'I was angry with my friend. I told my wrath. My wrath did end.' What was good enough for the luminary artist and philosopher Mr B is good enough for us.

Dealing with inequalities and envy

Some of your friends will have more money than you; some will have less. You may not all have equally success- ful careers. One of you may have what the other would dearly love: great family, house, fab figure, interesting job, vibrant lifestyle, entertaining social life, holiday homes in – okay, we'll stop it there. Whoever you are, we hate you. Not really. Just a bit …

Acknowledge the different hands which life deals us. There is no need to feel apologetic or embarrassed about your good fortune or lack of it. Think about the occasions when this type of inequality is likely to become obvious – in the exchanging of presents or hospitality, for example, or in choices about holidays or entertainment – and prepare to handle the situation.

Regardless of which end of the scale you are, bring up the issue right at the beginning and, if necessary, indicate where you stand.

Useful phrases:

+ *'Is that about the right price range for everyone?'*

+ *'That's a great idea, but probably a little over-budget for me. Has anyone tried the new place on the high street?'*

+ *'I'd like to pay for the wine – no arguments!'*

Split loyalties

Shifts in partnerships and allegiances can cause friendships to crack under the strain. If necessary, you can be assertive about your position without taking sides:

'I won't be at the party on Saturday. At the moment, I'd rather not see John/Julia.'

Or:

'I'm not comfortable about that situation, so I'd rather not talk about it.'

Saying no to a friend

Remember you are saying no to the request and not rejecting the person. Friendships thrive on honesty and mutual understanding. Telling a friend when you really don't want to do something shows respect for you both and prevents the friendship being marred by issues of obligation and resentment.

PICTURE THIS

A friend has been staying with you while she gets back on her feet after a marriage break-up. She is feeling better, but is showing no sign of moving out. You have got room to accommodate her, but you would like her to leave.

TRY THIS

'Jacqui, I'm so pleased that you came to us when you needed to. It's great that you're making such good progress. The thing is, I think it's time now that you found a place of your own.'

When Jacqui bursts into tears and says she doesn't think she could cope by herself and she cannot believe you are throwing her out, say something like 'I know it's another change and it must seem daunting but I've thought it over and I really think it would be better all round if you make a different living arrangement. It will be good to enjoy visiting each other.'

Then, of course, you can offer to help her find somewhere or anything else that you can do to help. (Probably best to hold back on the offer to help her pack ...)

PICTURE THIS

A friend who is upset about something phones late at night and wants to talk. You are tired and want to go to bed.

TRY THIS

Don't let the conversation get going. Say right away, 'I do want to hear all about it, but we need to find a better time when I can really concentrate on what you're saying.' Then make whatever suggestion suits and agree a time when you'll both be free.

If you are the one phoning for a chat, it is always a good idea to ask if this is a good time. What is convenient for you may not work for everybody. You know what it is like when you are pouring your heart out and realise that the other person is only half-paying attention, trying to get something in the oven or helping kids with homework at the same time. The gracious thing for both parties is to check that the moment is convenient.

Out and about

Trains, boats and planes ... and buses and cars ...

In the days long before any of us graced the planet, getting from a to b may have been a more leisurely and romantic venture. Think of steamer trunks and steam engines, the Grand Tour of Europe, carriage and pairs, the glamour of the open road, the romance of railway stations, Trevor Howard saying a manly selfless goodbye to Celia Johnson after their brief encounter.

Being in close proximity to our fellow human beings and feeling anxious and under pressure tends to bring out the worst in us. You will cope more effectively with travel situations if you don't expect them to operate smoothly and if you decide not to let the inevitable blips and inconveniences affect you. When something bothers you so much that you want to make a request or a complaint, muster all your assertive skills and do so politely and firmly.

PICTURE THIS

You think a taxi driver is taking a longer than necessary route.

TRY THIS

Say something like 'I'm wondering if you have a reason for choosing this route?'

If you do not get a satisfactory reason, try something like 'I believe the High Street route is more direct – I'd like to go that way, please.'

PICTURE THIS

Someone is speaking loudly on his or her phone in the quiet compartment of the train.

TRY THIS

Choose your response according to the situation. If you can, just catch the person's eye and gesture to the 'Quiet' notice. If you need to speak, say something like 'Excuse me, you might not realise this is a quiet carriage.' If it is clear that the person is not going to stop, you might feel like grabbing the phone and ramming it down their throat (oh dear, the red mist is very near the surface, isn't it), but it is best to accept that you cannot force them to do so. You may decide to move seats, in which case you could say as you leave, 'I'm sorry you won't cooperate and I'm going to sit somewhere else.'

No, you shouldn't have to, but just tell yourself the person behaving so rudely lacks your advantages of grace and consideration for others.

Shops and services

It's OK to return faulty goods. It's also OK to return goods that are *not* faulty. It's OK to complain about bad service. It's also OK to thank someone for *good* service.

There are accepted and understood rhythms to the buying and exchanging of items and services, which are supported by legal and written policies. You can perform your role in these transactions pleasantly and firmly, without on the one hand feeling too timid to speak up or on the other hand coming across like a shrill spoilt diva.

Making a complaint

No matter what your complaint is about, prepare an assertive script to help you deliver it effectively. Decide the outline of what you will say and make your approach only when you can do so calmly.

Don't pile straight in demanding to see the manager or to have your money back. Greet the salesperson or the receptionist and say that you have a problem you would like to be resolved.

State the cause of your complaint.

Say what you want to happen: 'So I would like my money back/to replace this item/the work to be done again.'

Wait for a response.

If the person you are dealing with cannot or does not give you a satisfactory response, say: 'Is there someone else who could help me with this?'

Negotiating

When you are negotiating work to be done, such as a kitchen or shelves being built or a garden being tidied up, an assertive approach will get you the best service. This doesn't mean making demands, but being clear about what you want and where the possibilities for flexibility, if any, lie. Use phrases such as 'What I'd like is/What I need is' and follow with 'How can we go about getting that?'

Making a request

You want to ask your doctor to tell you again what is the cause of your symptoms because you didn't take it in properly the first time; you want to discuss a problem with your child's teacher; you want the person in the box office to check the availability of several dates.

There is no need to feel embarrassed or awkward, and there is no need to grovel. Any request you make is perfectly okay, so pitch it pleasantly and firmly. Make sure your 'sorry', which you will undoubtedly say, is a courtesy and not an abject apology.

If you need more time or a more convenient moment, say so. It is a good idea to offer two options yourself: 'When would be a good time for us to discuss this, three o'clock this afternoon or ten o'clock tomorrow morning?'

Assertive approaches to tricky situations in your work life

Becoming the boss of a friend

This is what promotion can do. Overnight, you stop being one of the girls who knows about each other's duvet days, sickies, long lunch breaks for crucial shopping or personal maintenance, who cover for each other's hungover or heartbroken under-performances, who always know the hottest gossip, and you become the person in charge.

How you handle the situation depends on the nature of your friendship, your management style and your friend's attitude to your new position.

The challenge is to balance your valued friendship with the demands of the job. This requires you to make some choices and set up some boundaries, and to communicate these appropriately. Don't just sit back and think that things will work out – they won't.

As soon as you can, have a chat with your friend about how you are both going to deal with the situation. Say something like 'I feel it's important that we don't let the work stuff interfere with our friendship. Let's figure out how we are going to manage it.'

However, you might hit the odd rocky patch.

PICTURE THIS

Your friend thinks that the rules that apply to everyone else don't apply to her.

TRY THIS

'You know what, Kerry, it's important that we all follow the agreed procedures. No exceptions, eh?'

PICTURE THIS

Your friend says something like 'That's not fair, you had loads of time off whenever your kids were sick.'

TRY THIS

'The thing is, Kerry, we're not talking about the past, we're dealing with the present situation.'

Actually, if she behaves like this, might you want to re-evaluate the friendship?

When your friend becomes your boss

It would be a good thing to take the initiative here. Congratulate your friend on the promotion and say (lightly) that you are sure your friendship will survive it. This shows you are aware that something will shift as a result of the new circumstance and indicates you will deal with it sensitively.

The same applies if you both went for the job and your friend got it.

If you are inwardly seething with resentment and hoping your mate will mess it up big time, get a grip! Acknowledge your feelings and move on. You might not feel okay about it until you are promoted yourself. You might need to leave or join a different team. It is your problem, so find a solution.

Someone taking credit for your work

Decide how big a deal it is and how much it matters to you. Give some thought also as to whether this is something that should be dealt with between you and the person concerned or if a more public readjustment is required.

In this kind of situation, a light touch may work best. If the claim is made publicly, depending on the context, you could say something like '*Whose* idea, Tom?' or 'Maybe not *quite* all your own work, Tom,' and laugh it off. This alerts other people to Tom's duplicity and makes you look as if you are rising above it.

Another strategy would be to add a comment which includes yourself, such as 'Yes, we thought it would work well, didn't we, Tom?' or 'Yes, if you remember, Tom, that was your first question when I came up with the idea.'

If an important issue is at stake or if this is something that happens frequently, you need to have a one-to-one. Express your feelings about the situation, and say what you would like to happen:

'Tom, I was angry/upset/surprised when you claimed that getting the Armstrong account was all your doing. If you remember, I had several significant meetings with them that contributed to the success. I'd like you to send Jane an email making this clear/I'm going to send Jane an email making this clear.'

Or:

'Tom, reality alert! That new system you claimed to have devised was all my doing, as you know. Now, are *you* going to make this clear to Jane, or am *I*?'

Here's a thought: you could get your own back by pretending to be your boss while she is away and stealing her job and her lover – oh, okay, hands up, Melanie Griffith got there first in *Working Girl* (1988) …

Asking for a rise or promotion

Even smart girls are bad at doing this. All the old ideas about how it is wrong to put yourself forward and how people will think that you are hard and grasping flood back and turn you into a whimpering, simpering piece of fluff who thinks that she doesn't deserve to be adequately rewarded for her work.

You need to straighten out your thinking and recognise that asking for tangible recognition goes with being in the working world. You are not being pushy, you are being responsible and realistic and doing what your male counterparts do without the slightest hesitation.

Make your case, to yourself first of all

Know your value in whatever marketplace you work in. You will have value by virtue of the role and position you hold, and by your individual strengths and talents. If you don't already know, find out what people in similar positions to you earn. Look at job adverts or ask at recruitment agencies. Make sure you are pitching in the right ballpark.

Get your evidence together. You need to be able to demonstrate in concrete terms everything you have done and achieved that merits reward.

Prepare for a refusal. You might get an outright 'no', you might get a request for time to consider it. Decide what you will say in either situation. Sulking or threatening is not an option. Practise a gracious 'thank you' and a request to discuss the matter again in, say, six months. You could also ask if there is anything you could or should do in the meantime to support your request.

Present your case

You need to present your case to the right person. Talk to the person who can make the decision. It is no good expecting someone to put in a good word for you, and in any case, you don't want your carefully prepared request to be diluted by an intermediary party.

Get the timing right

Before you make your approach, think about the current climate and atmosphere at work. If you know that things are economically tight, that redundancies have been made or that an expected order or commission has fallen through, now might not be a good time.

In the run-up to making your request, work on your own profile and reputation. You will strengthen your case if your boss knows, and other relevant people know, that you have made a successful presentation or had a good sales run, that you have come up with a great idea or managed a difficult situation with tact and diplomacy.

You might feel that knowing you do a good job should be enough – but it isn't. You need to bring an element of strategy into play and make sure that your commitment and your contribution are visible.

Use your knowledge and observation of your boss to choose the best time of day. When is he or she in the most receptive mood – morning, afternoon, after seeing particular clients, late in the week, early in the week?

Face to face

Make an appointment for a one-to-one interview. Even if you know the person well and there are opportunities to make an informal approach, there are many advantages to putting your request in a business-like framework.

Don't say what the meeting is for – that way, you give an opportunity for someone to think up all the reasons not to agree.

Going back after maternity leave

Don't just hope for the best. Your personal world has changed, and you will find the world of work to which you are returning has changed as well. Someone has been doing your job, perhaps someone who hoped you wouldn't return. Relationships will have shifted, new allegiances formed. You may need to learn the workplace politics and procedures all over again.

And, of course, your place in the pecking order has shifted. People will see you differently. They may view you as someone not quite in the swim of things. Naturally you want to put them right and to reclaim your rightful place, but give some thought as to how you do this, then take some proactive assertive steps. Don't wait for your first day back. In the few weeks before your return, meet the appropriate colleagues so that you can get up to date on the need-to-knows. When you start, you might want to take it gently for the first few weeks and suss out the situation.

You might have to deal with comments that tell you how great your replacement was or with comments about how rubbish he or she was. Treat both with care. Swallow your hurt pride or your secret pleasure and make a noncommittal reply like 'Interesting. Well, I'm back now and …'

Be gracious with whoever replaced you. Thank them and ask constructive questions about their plans.

Walk the line between awareness and oversensitivity. In your anxiety not to be seen as someone whose brains have turned to mush you might interpret harmless comments as derogatory. At the same time you may well have to deal with colleagues who don't seem to have grasped the fact that you are back, alive and kicking.

PICTURE THIS

A colleague keeps making references such as 'Of course, that was when you were away' or 'I suppose things have moved on since you were last here.'

TRY THIS

Meet this kind of comment with agreement, followed by a question:

'That was when I was away. Is it something I need to know about now?'

'Yes, things have moved on in all kinds of ways. I think I'm up to speed with most of the developments here. Is there anything specific you feel I should know?'

CHAPTER NINE

Dealing with Difficult People

Sometimes people are slow to take their cue from your fabulous assertive behaviour and remain stuck in a style that prevents them from enjoying the benefits of a different approach. Poor them! Show them the way by responding assertively to whatever they do and refusing to play their game.

If you want to change the dynamic of a relationship or situation, you can choose an appropriate strategy. What strategy you use depends on the particular circumstances, and you can choose the level and intensity of your response.

If the situation demands more than a quick-fix solution, plan your move carefully and give it time to work. Instant makeovers are for television. You cannot change a person by slapping on a coat of paint or war paint – no disrespect to the girls and boys who show us how to make a hovel into a palace and a rag into an *haute couture* dress. You cannot change a person at all. All you can do is change your own behaviour and watch the ripple effect.

How to handle a bulldozer

Pushy, aggressive people expect to be able to force you into submission, and we have all let that happen to us. Sometimes we feel it would take too much effort to stand up to them and it wouldn't get us anywhere, or we just feel a bit frightened or intimidated. And so we let them win and the template for future encounters is established.

At its worst extreme, this kind of behaviour is outright bullying. If this happens at work, you should first speak informally to a manager or supervisor. Keep a diary and copies of relevant incidents and communication. The next step, if necessary, would be to make a formal complaint.

In our personal lives, we can experience aggression through people's sharp speech, low-key pushing or in-your-face behaviour that results in our feeling flattened and got-at.

How to recognise if you are being bulldozed

See if any of the following apply to you:

+ You are shouted at, or spoken to more forcefully than the situation warrants.

+ You are the subject of putdowns and demeaning comments.

✦ You feel scared.

✦ You feel pushed into a corner so that you have to do what is being asked.

✦ You feel threatened.

✦ You feel that you are always in the wrong with someone.

✦ You feel humiliated.

✦ You feel that you are treated unfairly.

Strategies for handling a bulldozer

1. Tell the person you don't like their behaviour

Describe the behaviour and say it is unacceptable. Don't be too detailed about how it affects you but use a blanket phrase such as 'I don't like it.'

PICTURE THIS

Someone raises his or her voice to intimidate you.

TRY THIS

Raise your hand in a 'Stop' gesture and say, 'Zoe, you're shouting at me, and I don't like it.'

PICTURE THIS

Someone keeps on at you to sign up for a charity fun-run. You have already said no, but they are persisting.

Say something like, 'You know, Di, I've already said no, and nothing has changed. Please stop asking me.'

If she says something like 'Everyone else is doing it' or 'We really need the support', say, 'That may be, but my answer is no.'

2. Ask the person to explain their words or behaviour

Returning the ball into the other person's court is a great way of making them think about what they are doing or saying.

You say that you have changed your mind about a certain issue. Someone who you feel often has a go at you says, 'That's just typical of you.'

You ask, 'I wonder what you mean by that, Alina?'

If Alina says 'Nothing', just add, 'That's all right then.'

If Alina says something like 'You're always changing your mind', just ask, 'Am I? Does that bother you?'

3. Deal with offensive jokes or comments

If you feel angry or uncomfortable with someone's language or conversation, let them know. Don't think that you have to laugh or pretend it is all right: if you do this, you are making yourself a victim.

PICTURE THIS

Someone continually uses terminology that you find unacceptable.

TRY THIS

You could try a light approach: shake your head and say something like 'Not a great phrase, Harry. Try again.'

If nothing changes, be more direct: 'You know what, Harry, I find your use of that word unacceptable. Please, stop using it.'

How to handle a pushover

There is always the obvious option: push them over. After all, if someone goes around with a label on their forehead saying 'Kick me', it is only polite to do as they ask, isn't it?

The trouble is, this turns you into a person you don't want to be, someone who exploits and takes advantage of another's weakness. You will preserve your self-respect and show respect for a pushover's choices if you behave in a way that encourages them to express feelings, opinions and preferences.

If you allow yourself to become irritated or impatient, or find that you are controlling a situation more than you want to, you are actually turning into a victim of someone's passiveness.

How to recognise if you are a pushover's victim

See if any of the following apply to you:

+ You feel frustrated by their behaviour.

+ You feel helpless.

+ You keep interrupting someone.

+ You are tempted to or you do take advantage of someone's indecisiveness.

+ You are tempted to or you do take advantage of someone's inability to say no.

+ You don't listen to what they say.

+ You don't take their feelings seriously.

+ You hold back from making suggestions.

Strategies for handling a pushover

1. Bring your frustration into the open
Tell the person you feel frustrated, annoyed or helpless when he or she behaves in a certain way.

PICTURE THIS

Someone always says yes when you ask him or her to do you a favour, and you feel that sometimes they agree when they would rather not.

TRY THIS

Say something like 'You always say yes when I ask, and I'm very grateful for that, but I feel that sometimes you would rather say no. I'd really like you to say no when it isn't convenient for you.'

2. Offer the scale of 1–10

You can help someone to express a preference by giving them a structure on which to hang their reply. Giving a number to the strength of a feeling is a useful way to identify it and an easy way to communicate it.

PICTURE THIS

Someone always says he or she doesn't mind when you ask which restaurant they would like, if you should designate a driver or share a taxi or if they'd prefer tea or coffee.

TRY THIS

Suggest you each give a thumbs-up or down on a scale of 1–10, with 10 being totally in favour and 1 being totally against. Everyone displays fingers to show their number. Where you take it from there is up to you, but you will have observed that some kind of preference is being stated. Be sure to make the top end of your scale an odd number or someone might always go for the middle.

3. Be specific

Phrase your suggestions or questions in a way that antici-pates a positive response. This makes a 'don't mind' reply more difficult and encourages the person to make a decision of some kind.

So, instead of asking 'What day suits you?', ask: 'Is Thursday or Friday better for you?' Instead of asking 'What colour should we paint the living room?', ask: 'Should we go bright or neutral?'

You may still get a 'don't mind' but, having planted suggestions, you have something to work on.

How to handle a snake

One of the worst things about being given the run-around by a snake is it takes some time to realise you have been suckered. One of the reasons for this is that every time you feel you are being controlled or taken for a ride, the other person does or says something which makes you think you must be wrong. It is uncanny how they just seem to know the right moment to do this.

When you do wise up to the situation, you may start indulging in some self-flagellation about how you could have been so stupid. Stop that right now. Falling victim to a clever manipulator does not mean you are stupid – but letting it continue might suggest you are being less than smart. Allowing somebody to pull your strings, even in comparatively harmless contexts, weakens your self-respect. Sandie Shaw, with her bare feet and her lovely swinging bob, may have won the Eurovision Song Contest with a song about being a Puppet on a String (check it out on YouTube) but she later called the song 'sexist drivel'. Straight talking, Sandie!

How to recognise if you are being manipulated

See if any of the following apply to you:

+ You feel confused about what someone wants.

+ You feel someone is taking advantage of you.

+ You feel the spotlight is constantly turned back on the other person and his or her feelings and experiences.

+ You feel the relationship is unbalanced.

+ You are always trying to please and placate the other person.

+ You have to keep searching your memory or checking your diary to check when certain things were said and done.

+ You feel resentful.

+ You make excuses for the other person – after all, he or she means well/is having a hard time/had an unhappy childhood.

Strategies for handling a snake

1. Bring the game out into the open
Show that you recognise the tactics that are being used.

Make an assertive statement that is open and straightforward and gets to the heart of the matter.

PICTURE THIS

You decide to address the fact that one of the things your snake-like person frequently does is offer to help, then just doesn't follow through.

TRY THIS

So you say, 'You know, Josh, I appreciated your offer to support me at the meeting, and I understand that you didn't show because you had the date down wrongly but I actually feel you never had any intention of turning up.'

2. Don't get hooked in

Be prepared to have your words turned back on you. A skilled manipulator may well blame you for thinking he or she would ever behave that way: 'How could you think that? I'm really hurt that you have such a low opinion me' or 'There must be something wrong with you if that's what you think.'

The reply may be accompanied by a flounce-out or tears. And what might you do? Rush in to reassure, to justify, to apologise. And there you are, back under control. You have taken the bait.

You need to remain strong and say something like 'That's what I think' or 'That's how it looks to me' and refuse to be drawn in any further.

3. Refuse to let your buttons be pushed

Recognise what your buttons are. If you are anxious to be liked and to please people, if the approval of others is very important to you, if you are scared of argument and confrontation or if you feel insecure, you are an easy target for a snake.

4. Listen to your gut instinct

Trust your feelings rather than what the person says – and focus on the actions, not the words, of the other person.

Don't accept an insincere apology. Don't get drawn into discussion.

CHAPTER TEN

·

Praise and Compliments

You probably think nice things about people all the time. You notice someone's new outfit looks great. You think how tactfully your colleague handled that really difficult customer, how he kept his cool and defused the situation. You think how well your sister, your friend or your daughter is coping with bringing up her children by herself. You admire your son-in-law's determination in sticking at his degree course although he is finding it tough going.

These thoughts and impressions flit through our minds and more often than not don't make it to our mouths. We hold back from expressing our appreciation, our pleasure and our approval.

The reasons for this are mainly to do with awkwardness and self-consciousness. When we give this kind of positive recognition, we are taking a step outside our comfort zone and making or consolidating a personal connection in a direct and vibrant way that can have a powerful effect on us and the other person. We excuse ourselves for not taking this step by claiming that it would be embarrassing or misinterpreted.

We diminish the potential effect by telling ourselves that the comment would be seen as insincere or patronising and talk ourselves out of ever paying a compliment by claiming that we'd just be making the other person feel awkward as well.

What's the worst that can happen? Someone will hate you for ever and ever for daring to like or admire something about them? As if. OK, at first you might sound stilted or clumsy. You might feel weird but you can learn how to do this effectively, you know you can. It only takes a bit of practice before you are communicating your approval with clarity and sincerity.

Looking for and responding to what is bright and positive about people and their behaviour will have a positive effect on you and make you feel engaged with the communities you are part of. Then there you are, making someone else feel good and feeling the love from the upbeat vibe this generates.

What kind of praise or compliment?

Focus on something the person does or says. Whatever is good will be something about his or her behaviour, what qualities it displays and the positive effect it has. So if you want to make a complimentary remark about someone's appearance, pinpoint an aspect of the person's self-presentation that reflects your perception that they have made effective choices with clothes, grooming, and so on.

Complimenting someone's eye colour or shapely nose is not giving positive recognition – although it may be quite nice for the person on the receiving end – because individuals are not responsible for these qualities. They are responsible for their own behaviour, and genuine praise celebrates this.

Don't confuse praise and thanks

Most of us are pretty good with our 'thank yous' and give and receive them many times a day. It is hard to buy a tube of mints without several expressions of thanks being exchanged. That's fine. The thing about 'thank you' is it has more impact when it isn't said than when it is: 'I went to all that trouble, and he didn't even say thank you.' Thanks are polite, thanks are an essential part of civilised behaviour, but thanking someone is not the same as praising them. 'Thanks for helping me out last night' is not the same as saying 'I was so impressed with the calm way you took control.'

When to praise or give a compliment

First of all, go by your gut feeling, that little warm kick you get when you are pleased, delighted or impressed by someone. Decide you are going to share your impression with the person concerned. Think about the appropriate time and place. Sometimes an immediate response is good, particularly if there may not be another suitable moment to say it. On other occasions, you may like to wait and give lengthier and more considered feedback.

Be specific

Praise or compliments of a general nature have a feel-good effect. If you focus on something specific, the effect is much more powerful because you demonstrate you have thought about exactly what it is that impresses you. Don't just say, 'You look nice today,' say, 'That colour really suits your complexion' or 'I like the way your new hairdo channels the Mad Men look.' Don't just say, 'That was a great talk,' say, 'I really enjoyed the anecdotes from your work overseas.' Instead of 'You did a great job tidying your bedroom,' say, 'The way you've arranged the books makes your room look very neat.'

If you can avoid general words such as 'nice' and 'good', your compliments will have much more impact

Linking

An effective way to give a great compliment is to link your thanks or your general observation with praise of something specific:

✦ *'Thanks for talking to Lou last night. You know, I love the way you are so generous with your time when someone is in need of help.'*

✦ *'You were terrific! Your great comic timing made that last scene a triumph.'*

✦ *'It was great of you to help Elly get ready for the prom. You made her hair look so lovely.'*

Keep the spotlight on the other person

Keep the attention on the other person. Don't turn it back on yourself by making a comparison like 'I couldn't have done such a good job.' This just encourages the recipient to rush in and reassure you, and then you engage in a frenzy of mutual backslapping which wipes out the effect of your compliment.

Don't involve anyone else, either, by making a comparison in favour of the person you are speaking to. If you say, 'You're a much better listener than Ben,' the other person may feel obliged to defend Ben, and suddenly there you are, talking about Ben, who shouldn't figure in this encounter at all.

Don't add anything negative

The song tells us to 'Accentuate the Positive,' an uplifting affirmation of every aspect of grown-up assertiveness, don't you agree? Bear this in mind when you praise someone.

This is not the moment for those little negative add-ons that manage to take away the good impact, even if they are not meant unkindly. We have all smarted from these comments: 'That was a delicious dinner you cooked us. Such a shame about Toni's tantrum.'

What does this make you think of? Toni's tantrum. The delicious dinner bit is lost.

You might think a few jokes would have made the talk even more enjoyable, that it is a pity there wasn't quite enough pudding to go round or that, if the diagrams had been clearer, the display would have been even better – but don't say so at this point. This is not the appropriate time or place. On the occasions when you judge that you do need to discuss negative aspects, do so in the right context.

Don't use praise to manipulate

It's tempting, isn't it! You say, 'Oh, you're such a great cook, Linda. Your pavlova is out of this world and no one makes it so well.' Then a short time afterwards, you say, 'Would you mind doing half a dozen pavlovas for the party?' Tempting – and actually pretty obvious. Find a more direct way of asking for meringue dishes.

Compliments at work

Sometimes we take each other for granted. People get on with the jobs they are paid to do and all too often the only shared feedback on a daily basis is critical. We might say positive things about colleagues in formal appraisal situations or when they leave, but that is no substitute for the kind of genuine, morale-boosting, approving comment which brings a lovely energy to the day, as well as providing a framework for growth and learning.

Focus on detail

Comment on what is specifically good about what the person has done. Notice the skills and attributes that contribute to what it is you like. They might be qualities such as patience, humour or helpfulness, courage, thoughtfulness or trustworthiness. They might be skills such as technical expertise, problem-solving abilities, clear thinking, artistic ability or practical skills.

Where appropriate, make the detail you comment on relevant to the context. Relevance here means the aspect that makes a difference. For example, if you are in a situation where the wording of a written reply is important and someone produces a very well expressed letter, don't say, 'Good work getting that out so quickly.'

Be sincere

You will be spotted a mile off if you say nice words to butter someone up, to keep him or her off your back or to make yourself seem great for noticing (yes, that's you, Ms Manipulator).

Who do you praise?

Everyone who earns it. You can go across, up and down the food chain. We are all human, and we all like and need recognition.

Family and friends

We often forget those nearest and dearest to us will also respond to some genuine, specific praise. We take it for granted they know they are loved and appreciated, and we say nice things formally at occasions like weddings, big birthdays and retirements – and funerals, when it is too late.

Take some time to think about what you value in those close to you – then find an opportunity to tell them.

PICTURE THIS

A friend or family member always texts you good luck with the work pitch or the dentist, meeting the significant other's children for the first time or the hospital appointment. You always text back 'Thanks.'

TRY THIS

Say: 'It's so great to know that you're thinking of me.'

People who help

It is delightful to receive good service, and it is a good thing to let people know when they have delighted you. Go a step further than the genuine thanks which you always give and offer genuine focused feedback.

PICTURE THIS

You are looking for the best deal on a new phone. The assistant listens to what you need and talks you through a range of suitable options.

TRY THIS

'Thanks for your advice. Your product knowledge was very helpful, and I really appreciate the way you listened and understood my needs.'

PICTURE THIS

Your teenager is very shy and is reluctant to speak up in class, although he has a lot to offer. One of his teachers sees his potential and encourages him to be more forthcoming.

TRY THIS

'Thanks for helping Ollie. He's much more confident now. It's great that you spotted what he has to offer.'

Take it further

It would only take a matter of minutes to send an email or make a phone call to pass on your positive observation. We manage to find the time to make our complaints heard, so why not share our gratitude, approval and admiration as well?

Strangers

Yes, we know this sounds as if you will be getting yourself into a whole load of trouble, but just think about it. You say thank you to someone who opens a door for you, makes room for you or picks up something you have dropped. It is probably an automatic thank you, maybe muttered as you go on your way.

You can turn these brief encounters from black and white to Technicolor with just a couple of tweaks. All you have to do is smile as you say it and make the briefest of eye contact. If the circumstances are appropriate, add something like 'That's thoughtful of you' or 'I appreciate that.'

You could take it a little further and give a compliment to a stranger. If you pass a garden that looks lovely and the owner is there, why not just say so? If you admire the boots that the woman next to you in the queue is wearing, you could just say, 'Great boots, by the way.'

Get the timing right for these – what works is giving the compliment as you pass or as you leave, unless you want to engage in further conversation about spring flowers or the ankle- versus full-length-boot debate, which might also work.

Won't they feel great? Won't you feel great for saying it rather than just thinking it?

Receiving praise or a compliment

Many of us are not good at this. We feel embarrassed, we feel it is big-headed to be pleased, and we don't know how to react. Often, our instinct is to rebuff the comment and diminish it, thinking that this is the only acceptable way to respond.

You are praised for the success of a project that you headed. You say, 'Oh, it wasn't just me, it really was a team effort.' Cue an Oscar-style recitation of everyone who helped you, including your inspirational godmother and your cat.

A friend remarks that your skirt looks very stylish. You say, 'It's really old' or 'Only 50p from such-and-such shop.'

Your family praises your Chinese stir-fry. You say, 'All that chopping took me hours' or 'Don't get too used to it, it's fish fingers for the rest of the week.'

Imagine the positive comment is a present that someone is giving you. In the same way you choose a birthday present carefully with the recipient's taste in mind, someone has chosen something good about you and picked the words to describe the effect of your wonderfulness. This person has then done the equivalent of wrapping up the present attractively and has presented it to you.

What have you done? You have thrown it right back at them. You have dismissed the thought and effort that went into the gift. Your rejection may hurt the other person. Your behaviour may have the effect of making the giver feel foolish for having bothered. You are questioning the giver's judgement and the giver's taste. You are not behaving graciously.

If you want to give credit for other people who helped you with something you are being praised for, of course you should do so. The right time and place is not when you personally are being praised for your contribution. At this moment, the gift is being presented to you. It is discourteous to insist straight away on sharing it.

Accepting praise and compliments in the spirit in which they are offered is an assertive skill that benefits you and others.

What to say

The first thing you say is 'Thank you'. Look pleased as you say it and meet the other person's eyes. Don't flutter your eyelashes or look coy – and definitely no squirming in embarrassment. Accept the gift graciously in the spirit in which it is offered. Keep your response brief, but add something like 'I'm glad you liked it', 'I appreciate that' or 'That's so good to hear'.

Make sure your comment is positive. You can add something specific to the context:

+ *'I'm pleased you thought it went well – I spent a long time preparing.'*

+ *'Glad you think the colour works – it's one of my favourites.'*

+ *'I was pleased to be able to help.'*

+ *'Thank you for saying that. It's made me feel good/made me feel it's been worthwhile/made me determined to carry on/made my day.'*

Don't return it

You might feel you want to say something nice in return – that's great, but don't do it straightaway. Your compliment will not be seen as authentic but as a tit-for-tat return given because you feel that is the right thing to do. Your warm reception of someone's praise is, in its way, a compliment to him or her. There will be a suitable opportunity for you to be complimentary at a later point.

If there will not be another opportunity, wait until a little later in the conversation and comment on an aspect of the person's behaviour which is in a different category. If someone is complimentary about your appearance, you could say something nice about the conversation you have had – they have made you laugh or made you think, or you enjoyed hearing their opinion of the film.

When to ask for more – yes, really

Unspecific praise

When someone praises you in a general way, it is absolutely okay to ask for something specific. Don't worry, it is not like saying 'Oh, go on, tell me much more about how wonderful I am'. It is making an enquiry which shows that you appreciate the comment and would like to benefit from the observation.

This is particularly so in a work situation when someone tells you, 'You did a great job there' or 'I don't know what we'd do without you.' No harm at all in saying, 'Thanks, that's good to hear. Could you tell me, what did you find particularly helpful?' When he or she tells you, just finish the encounter with 'Thanks. That's very helpful/ I appreciate that.'

Double-edged compliments

When you are not sure of the intention behind a compliment, say you appreciate the comment, but are not sure if you've understood it. That's always nice to hear – right? This is a good strategy when you don't quite trust the speaker's motives. Listen to your instinct that detects perhaps a masked put-down or disapproval masquerading as praise.

Reply in a way which takes ownership of the encounter and which doesn't fall into the trap, if there is one.

PICTURE THIS

Someone eyes you up and down and says, 'You're looking very well!'

Now, you as a confident grown-up with adequate self-esteem do not immediately think this means you look too fat or too thin. You do not turn everything into a body-shape issue. But you weren't quite comfortable with the person's tone and expression.

TRY THIS

'Am I? Thank you!' (said with delight)

'What makes you say that?'

'I've been trying the healthy lifestyle thing – so thank you for noticing!' (said with delight)

PICTURE THIS

You are not a great cook, but you rustle up a passable meal for a family group. Your partner's mother says, 'Absolutely delicious, Nigella!'

Hmm. Is she getting at me?

TRY THIS

'Glad you enjoyed it! What was particularly to your taste?'

Put it in writing

We are old school about this one. Emails and texts are great, particularly when you want to say a quick 'thank you'. But we are talking real writing, with a pen (yes, you do know what a pen is). A written thank-you note is a pleasure to receive because it shows that you have made an effort. And even more pleasurable to give and to receive is a note which praises us or compliments us.

You don't have to wait for a specific incident to give someone positive acknowledgement, although a particular occasion can provide a way in.

If you admire the way your daughter manages to hold down a demanding job and give her children time and attention, let her know. You could take the opportunity when one of the kids has achieved success in something at school or an occasion when you have spent some time with them all. Write a note which says how nice it was to hear about Zach's exam/see Charlotte in the school play/ spend last Sunday with them all and goes on to say something like 'I'd like to tell you …' or 'You have …', followed by specific words of praise for what she has done and is doing.

That is what being a smart girl is all about. It is about being great to yourself and being great with others.

A final word on handles and handling

Dealing with, handling, managing, coping – hmm. You might think these words sound, you know, a bit hard, a bit rough, a bit mechanical. But they are words that express the process of forming and building relationships, and our connections and interactions with people cannot be left to chance. They need thought and attention. They need handling.

A girl who learnt this was Katy Carr, heroine of the 19th-century children's classic *What Katy Did*. Bedridden after an accident, she learns lessons in the School of Pain, one of which is that everything, everybody in the world has two handles. If you find the smooth handle, things work out easily. If you take hold of the rough handle – yes, you've got it!

King Arthur in the musical *Camelot* asked, 'How to handle a woman?' And guess what he was told – not to flatter or threaten, brood or make like a big romancer. The only way, the wise old man told him, is to love her, simply love her.

That's it. Be nice to people. Feel the love.